Successor journal to *Theatre Quarterly* (1971-1981)
VOLUME VIII   NUMBER 32   NOVEMBER 1992

NTQ
NEW THEATRE QUARTERLY

Contents

*New Theatre Quarterly is published in February, May, August, and November by Cambridge University Press, The Edinburgh
Building, Shaftesbury Road, Cambridge CB2 2RU, England*   ISBN 0 521 42943 9   ISSN 0266-464X

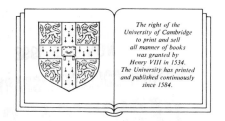

The right of the
University of Cambridge
to print and sell
all manner of books
was granted by
Henry VIII in 1534.
The University has printed
and published continuously
since 1584.

CAMBRIDGE UNIVERSITY PRESS

The Pitt Building, Trumpington Street, Cambridge CB2 1RP
40 West 20th Street, New York, NY 10011-4211, USA
10 Stamford Road, Oakleigh, Victoria 3166, Australia

Editorial Enquiries: Great Robhurst, Woodchurch, Ashford, Kent TN26 3TB, England

Unsolicited manuscripts are considered for publication in New Theatre Quarterly. *They should be sent to Simon Trussler at the above address, but unless accompanied by a stamped addressed envelope (UK stamp or international reply coupons) return cannot be guaranteed. Contributors are asked to follow the journal's house style as closely as possible.*

Advertising: Enquiries should be sent to the Journals Promotion Department at Cambridge or to the American Branch of Cambridge University Press.

Subscriptions: *New Theatre Quarterly* (ISSN: 0266-464X) is published quarterly by Cambridge University Press, The Edinburgh Building, Shaftesbury Road, Cambridge CB2 2RU, and The Journals Department, 40 West 20th Street, New York, NY 10011-4211.

Single parts cost £10.00 (US$17.00 in the USA and Canada) plus postage. Four parts form a volume. The subscription price (which includes postage) of Volume VIII, 1992, is £37.00 (US$66.00 in USA and Canada) for institutions, £21.00 (US$32.00) for individuals ordering direct from the publishers and certifying that the Journal is for their personal use.

Orders, which must be accompanied by payment, may be sent to a bookseller or to the publishers (in the USA and Canada to the American Branch).

Copies of the Journal for subscribers in the USA and Canada are sent by air to New York to arrive with minimum delay. Second class postage paid at New York, NY, and at additional mailing offices. POSTMASTER: send address changes in the USA and Canada to *New Theatre Quarterly*, Cambridge University Press, The Journals Department, 40 West 20th Street, New York, NY 10011-4211.

Claims for missing issues will only be considered if made immediately on receipt of the subsequent issue.

Typeset by L. Anderson Typesetting, Woodchurch, Ashford, Kent TN26 3TB, and printed and bound in Great Britain by the University Press, Cambridge.

Slawomir Mrozek

Theatre versus Reality

In 1988 the Polish playwright Slawomir Mrozek was invited by the Nobel Foundation and the Royal Theatre in Stockholm to deliver a speech for the 'Strindberg-O'Neill' symposium on the issues suggested by this title. In defining his terms and their relationship, he combined Aristotelian precision and existential candour with a gentle irony entirely his own. The speech was first printed in the Polish theatre journal *Dialog*, to whose editors we are grateful for permission to print this translated version.

I HAVE BEEN asked to talk about theatre as well as about reality. Fortunately, both topics are so vague that one cannot avoid banal generalities, which in this case will help to mask my complete ignorance about some aspects of both theatre and reality.

At first I found myself wondering what the title of the talk should be, because the request was not very specific. I was asked for something general – a few thoughts on reality and theatre, or maybe the other way round, on theatre and reality: the choice was left to me. I was also left to decide whether theatre with reality – or reality with theatre – were to be separated by 'versus' or bound together with 'and'.

I decided that 'theatre' should be mentioned first, and only then would I talk about 'reality' – which does not mean, of course, that I give a priority to such order. But if one cannot pronounce the two words simultaneously, it is obviously better to start with the less ambiguous one, which has many possible meanings anyway. A similar reason lies behind my choice of 'theatre versus reality' instead of 'theatre and reality', since by giving priority to 'and' at the expense of 'versus', I would have created an entirely false impression that, after all, theatre was more important to me.

To start with, I should probably give a full definition of both theatre and reality, but my confidence begins to dwindle whenever I have to talk on the subject of reality. Attempts to define what reality is have been made since we learned to formulate questions, and some people, much greater and

more important than myself, have spent their lives trying to resolve this problem. But so far the fruit of this mental effort has been meagre, although as with all heroic efforts the effort itself should be regarded with due respect. With theatre it seems to be entirely different, because we assume that all of us more or less realize what theatre is.

I am not suggesting that the choice of 'versus' instead of 'and' gives us a perfect solution. 'Versus' indicates implicitly that there is a qualitative rift between reality and theatre. I want to assure you that I do not think such a rift, break, difference, or anything similar worthy of our attention can be found between reality and theatre.

At this point however, you might be getting somewhat impatient with my deliberations, wondering what on earth I have been going on about and what according to me does or does not exist. Aware of your growing impatience, I shall try to speed up my mental processes in order to come up with something to salvage my little talk – and so, instead of 'theatre' I shall say 'stage' – a real, genuine stage made of wooden planks.

I hope this will be a fortunate swap, and one without sacrifice of meaning, because a stage means a theatre, since there is no theatre without a stage. A theatre can do without properly designed settings, scripts, or even without actors. Even, stretching our minds, we can create an imaginary spectacle on an empty stage. But the stage must be there – nothing can happen without it.

A stage is a tangible phenomenon. We see it and we can touch it if we like, so at last we have something more than a purgatory of pure ideas. This in turn will help us to clarify our concept of reality – because we can then assume that reality is everything which is not a stage and which does not take place on a stage. So we can say that reality begins somewhere behind the stage – in the wings, and stretching in concentric circles into an infinity known perhaps only to God himself. I realize that this is a gross simplification, and that a serious debate cannot be conducted with such simplistic concepts: but let us allow ourselves to lower the level of the discussion and admit at least some of these simplistic ideas. After all, it is better to sink low than to be stuck in a vacuum.

The first observation which comes to my mind when I am looking at an empty stage or at a theatre from which reality has crudely been whisked away is the ease with which theatre can be so easily extracted from its wider context yet still exist in its own right. A stage can simply exist and it exists simply by being where it is. When there is no stage there is something else instead, and that is it. The limits of a stage are clear and well defined: one can be either on a stage or off a stage, but never in between, because such an intermediate zone simply cannot exist.

With reality it is entirely different. Although it is obvious that reality begins where the stage ends, nobody really knows where are its limits. It is not even clear whether it has any limits at all. When confronted with such unmediated limitless reality in a pure or let us say naked form, we feel lost and rather helpless.

Now it is time we put the question: why do people need theatre? We assume, of course, that they do need it. But let us precede the word 'need' with a qualifying term 'still'. Why do people *still* need theatre? If one thinks about entertainment value, it is obvious that theatre lost out to 'show business' quite some time ago. The word 'business' suggests here that things are organized in such a way that a demanded product – a show or entertainment – should be supplied in a sufficient quantity. Theatre

as a supplier of entertainment has been outstripped by the movies, television has facilitated this defeat, and now video is trying to phase out all the remaining traces of theatrical life.

But if the entertainment value of theatre is today nearly non-existent, one wonders why theatre still exists at all. The fact that it does survive against all odds suggests that it must fulfil other needs – different from the need to be entertained.

Whenever we come into contact with a stage either by looking at it or by being physically present on it, we feel that at last we are saved from chaos: here is somewhere where the volatile forces of chaos can be kept at bay. On such occasions we are glad to enjoy some peace and a break from our daily nightmares. It is interesting that television is not able to offer us such a relief – in which respect television rather resembles reality than theatre.

In fact, in view of our assumption that everything which is not a stage belongs to reality, we may say that television and reality are one. Watching television we see a shapeless universe, a never-ending trivial chat show and a myriad of blinking pictures. All this can be compared to slices cut from a very thick, tasteless, and never-ending sausage, every slice of which tastes the same as the previous slice, with nothing to alleviate the monotonous quality.

If theatre is a place of refuge from overwhelming chaos, then lots of things which we tend to describe as theatrical have nothing to do with theatre. Let us take for instance the so called 'happening'. Not so long ago this was regarded as a highly theatrical phenomenon, but today it has lost some of its qualities. One does not need to go to theatre in order to see a 'happening'. Reality, life as a whole, we ourselves make up a constant happening. So why bother to go to the theatre for it? Why struggle in the traffic and spend the money on tickets?

Every moment on the street can give us a show, which the theatre can only try to reproduce on the stage. And we may be sure that the quality of a street show will be better, since no theatre can afford to transform the whole world into a stage and hire everybody to be actors on it. The quality of acting in a theatre will not surpass that of real life, either. A couple of chaps who are desperately trying to work out how to look genuine will never achieve life's authentic spontaneity. But even if we eventually go to the theatre to watch a happening, we shall realize that we are into something which we want to escape: a nonsensical reality – perhaps the nonsense of our own existence.

I hope you will not think that I have been so pigheadedly discussing happenings because I have something against them. Happenings simply lost their topicality, and a tirade against them would sound as outdated as the thing itself. We have new fashionable phenomena today, and I have looked at the happening only because it served as a good illustration of a general thesis. Many past, present, and future phenomena which for one reason or another are related to our unfortunate happening seem to have their origins in a general trend, much deeper than a simple drive to change everything around us, since it has a much more profound and much more universal dimension – the trend, I mean, to remove and iron out all differences. To wipe out the dividing line which separates the stage from the rest of the world is only one instance of this general tendency. This process is by no means new and we should not be surprised if it gets more conspicuous.

A stage is situated in both time and space, which means that it is also limited by them. But the word 'limited' has many negative connotations in Polish. It describes something inferior, or as the scientists would say 'pejorative'. So it would be better to say that the stage is neither situated nor limited but *placed* in time and space. Whatever happens on it has its beginning and end.

First of all, however, it has no consequences. It is unlike reality, where all actions have some immediate as well as future – sometimes entirely unpredictable – consequences. We can never be sure about the short and long-term consequences of our daily actions, nor do we know what actions may yet be triggered off by the results of what we have just accomplished. The thought that the chain of cause and effect may continue even after one's death is difficult to bear, since it is hard to accept that a chain of events started by us will last longer than ourselves. The whole idea seems paradoxical, because we are convinced that our end means the end of everything else.

In the theatre however, we always know what the ending is going to be like – assuming, of course, that we do not leave before the end of the play. And what is more, we may be sure that the show will not be continued. The end always means the end, the moment the actors quit the stage and we leave the theatre.

Action without consequence is no less tempting to us as than any other hazardous game. This temptation encourages us to play theatre, chess, cards, and whatever else we can think of. But the notion of a game is nearly parallel with the notion of play: in fact the two notions overlap with each other. Carnival, for instance, is a game, so is theatre, while snooker can be easily perceived as play. When we are playing a game, we are exercising the abilities and skills which a given game requires. But since every game imitates some natural action, by playing we are perfecting genuine skills – that is, we are learning how to live without having to think about the consequences of our actions.

Even the end of the game is an imitation. It imitates death or the end of all activity, so when the game is over we know that this is the end and that there is nothing beyond this ending. In real life, however, we cannot be sure whether there is life after death.

Action on the stage is finite, which means that it will never extend beyond the stage and that no external factor is capable of changing the course of theatrical action. This is like playing a game of cards, in which we always know the exact number of cards. We also know that the number of different combinations of cards may be infinite – whereas when we play life we never know what new cards will be thrown into the game nor do we know which of our own cards will be suddenly taken out of our hands.

This is why we always say that a game is fair while life is deceitful. When we lose or win a game we normally know the reasons, and we can analyze them in great detail. In real life we never know why we lose or why we win, and what is more we can never possess such knowledge, because the rules of life, unlike those of a game of cards, are never disclosed to us. Therefore we tend to suspect that life is not governed by rules.

Action on a stage gives us some metaphysical consolation. In life we long for order and to know the purpose of our existence, which somehow we are not able to identify. In moments of despair we accuse reality of being as chaotic and incoherent as only a madman's dream can be: yet in spite of this we keep turning out individual scenarios for our lives. Often these are convoluted, altered, and modified, yet we never give up on them. A day without even a tiny, most trivial, and carelessly drawn up scenario is not worth living.

When we go to the theatre and find out that it is possible to produce something which is well designed and holds together, we begin to believe that there is some purpose in life and that one day we shall be able to put together something equally coherent. It is undoubtedly true that such experience does help us to get on with our individual plans.

Every good play or well-acted episode convinces us that some order is feasible. And if it is feasible in theatre, then why should it not be feasible in real life? Why cannot the methods which are used in the theatre help us to sort out the problems of the universe?

If there is no proof that such methods would work in real life, equally there is no proof that such methods would not work. The argument saying that we know who prepared a given performance while we have no idea who created the universe has some weight, yet it cannot be taken as a final proof. In theatre we can see who prepared the performance, and we can see that there is an overall structure or unifying principle which holds together a number of smaller units, and that each of these units has its definite place and function within the greater structure.

The presence of an overall structure or of a major principle ensures that the units are not randomly scattered, but organized in a meaningful and coherent way. So even if a number of contemporary styles of theatre persist in conveying a message about the decomposition of the world, we seem to remain very composed. The reasons for this are clear: if a theatre wants to show to the public how the world is falling apart, then a number of people have to work closely together in order to organize a performance to convey total disorganization. Such a performance must be considered very carefully, and so the theoretically despised and rejected principles of coherence and integrity sneak in through the back door and become crucial in the preparation of a show intended to defy those very principles.

The temporal dimension of the performance helps us to understand our ordinary notion of time. In spite of the fact that we all use watches, our knowledge of the structure of time is limited. We know that 'something happens sometime', but we know neither what this 'sometime' consists of nor how its parts or structures are linked together.

Theatre encourages us to investigate these problems. In theatre, time is structured to reflect the action of a given play. It may be a day, a year, or any other unit of time, but it is almost never identical with the duration of a performance. Normally it is longer, but the slowed down action in the theatre of Robert Wilson shows that occasionally it may be shorter.

Now time which is determined by the action of a play contains many other kinds of time – time recollected or foreseen by the characters, or the time of their past which they have to consider, as well as the time of their future which will be determined by what is happening on the stage. The past is never directly available to us: we learn of it while listening to dialogues, or retrieve it from gestures and actions. The future may be seen only occasionally – thus we shall never see Chekhov's three sisters on their way to Moscow, even if they really decide to go there. What we are left with is the time of a performance, which serves as a vehicle for all the times included in a play. On most nights this time begins at 7.30 and ends around 9.45.

The complexity of the temporal dimension does not stop here, because every performance takes place on Tuesday or Friday or some other day in the week. It is always only one day – one space in a diary, which is shared both by the actors and the audience. But a performance may be given more than once or twice – indeed, normally there are tens or hundreds. So what are the implications of this repetition?

There are many. Can we for instance say with clear conscience and full conviction that Desdemona died only once, if on the stage she has died a hundred times? Can we say this, even if a given production of *Othello* is about to end after a hundred nights, and it seems that at last Desdemona's life has come to an end – yet we know at the same time that the play will be staged elsewhere again and again, and that each performance will take place only on a particular day in a particular week? So what will be our conclusions about Desdemona? That she always dies? That she does not die at all? Or maybe that she is a little bit dead and a little bit alive at the same time?

Thinking about time as it is conceived on the stage prepares us for dealing with time in real life. We can see now how our actions, which are firmly set in the present time, run parallel to the time of our memories, and are intertwined with our imaginary representations of the past. We can see how these two temporal dimensions are connected with the time we enter into while reading books or newspapers or listening to other people's stories, or with the time which is determined by rail and flight timetables. We can add to this the time of our psychic moods and our inner time – time which is measured by biological clocks ticking inside our bodies. And all these times are carefully supervised by the time of our clocks and our diaries.

It is sometimes said that theatre is merely a fictitious creation. So if Desdemona has never existed, it does not matter whether she died once, many times, or not at all. It is also said that theatre imitates life, and in this case theatre is given a slightly bigger role to play: however, it is still a role of secondary importance, because it is quite conceivable to imagine life without theatre, since we know that the existence of a genuine thing does not depend on the existence of its imitations. Theatre may exist, but reality can easily cope without it, so nothing will suffer if theatre goes. According to this theory theatre is only a model of reality, or a computer simulation of real events.

Finally there is the theory according to which theatre does not imitate life but is its representation. This last theory attaches to theatre much more importance than the previous ones by emphasizing the fact that representation does not mean imitation but analogy. If we accept this assumption, then Desdemona's death becomes an issue worthy of serious consideration.

But this is a potentially dangerous situation. We have agreed, of course, that the theatre represents life, and this remains clear. However, once we accept the notion of representation we cannot let it go when this question preys on our minds: if theatre represents life, what does life represent?

Some of us try to brush this question aside by saying 'life is just life and that's all'. But most of us are not satisfied with such a response: we want to know more. What if life is not self-sufficient? Or what if life is only a representation of something else? And what is this something else if it exists? This last question brings us to the edge of an intellectual precipice, which is not only unappealing but also turned upside down – because even if we were able to discover what life represents, we would have to find out in turn what this discovered representation was a representation of. A ghastly and endless hierarchical construction of representations begins to loom over our heads.

Should we, then, not ask any more questions, but return our debate to a more mundane level? Yet if we turn our eyes to more mundane aspects of representation, we find out that they are not simple, either.

If we assume that the phenomenon of representation does not exist, and everything around us is equally real, then we have to agree that theatre is neither a fiction, imitation, nor representation of reality, but a part of reality like everything else. In this case Desdemona's death has to be regarded as a real event, even if an actress who plays her on the stage sheds her costume after the performance and goes out to dinner.

At this point if we are not careful there may be a danger that we shall enter the realm of magical thought. But when does this danger emerge? Only if we assume in the first place that there is some vertical hierarchy of representation. If we accept the flat principle of analogy or convertibility of everything into everything else, we shall enter the realm of post-magical thought, and then even the poorest of shamans will give us the brush-off, because he will perceive our thinking as shallow, static, and unexciting, perhaps not thinking at all. And we may be sure that no magical thinking can be associated with such unappealing characteristics.

So only in the first case do we get close to magical thinking – one step more and we shall certainly be there. To achieve this we shall have to add the notion of correspondence to the previously accepted notion of analogy. As a result we shall achieve one indivisible but inwardly differentiated pan-reality – a pure case of irrationality and superstition.

So we should watch what we are doing, or where shall we be? In the company of those superstitious actors who believe that playing *Macbeth* brings on a curse? Or on a par with those theatregoers who used to beat up actors who played rogues and rascals because they were not able to see the difference between the two?

If we want to preserve our peace of mind, perhaps we had better not think about the relation of theatre to reality at all. Perhaps we'd better watch television.

Translated by Piotr Kuhiwczak

Steve Nicholson

Censoring Revolution: the Lord Chamberlain and the Soviet Union

In two earlier articles, Steve Nicholson has explored ways in which the the right-wing theatre of the 1920s both shaped and reflected the prevailing opinions of the establishment – in NTQ29 (February 1992) looking at how the Russian Revolution was portrayed on the stage, and in NTQ30 (May 1992) at the ways in which domestic industrial conflicts were presented. He concludes the series with three case studies of the role of the Lord Chamberlain, on whose collection of unpublished manuscripts now housed in the British Library his researches have been based, in preventing more sympathetic – or even more objective – views of Soviet and related subjects from reaching the stage. His analysis is based on a study of the correspondence over the banning of Geo A. DeGray's *The Russian Monk*, Hubert Griffith's *Red Sunday*, and a play in translation by a Soviet dramatist, Sergei Tretiakov's *Roar China*. Steve Nicholson is currently Lecturer in Drama at the Workshop Theatre of the University of Leeds.

IN MARCH 1918, the Lord Chamberlain's Office refused to license a melodrama. In the words of one of the readers who rejected the script,

It is probably only the first of many we shall get on this unsavoury subject, *raison de plus* to nip the movement in the bud.[1]

The Russian Monk was a dramatization of the life of Rasputin, but the implicit theme which merited such concern was the emergence of the Soviet Union and revolution.

Although there have been several assessments of censorship in the British theatre, none has focused primarily on the political aspects.[2] In January 1991 the papers and documents of the Lord Chamberlain relating to theatre censorship became freely available for consultation for the first time, and by drawing on this material and focusing on three plays which were refused licences, I shall argue that the significance of this area has been underestimated.

The Russian Monk was repeatedly rejected between 1918 and 1921, and never produced. *Red Sunday* was performed in a private club in 1929, but refused the licence which would have allowed it to transfer to a commercial theatre. *Roar China* was refused a licence in Britain in 1931, and its only private per-formance became the subject of government and police investigations. The files on these plays contain letters, documents, and comments which reveal much about the practical operation of censorship, the ideological basis on which it was founded, and the credit granted by the establishment to the theatre for influencing public opinion.

Successive Lord Chamberlains and their Examiners of Plays held that politics were not a suitable subject for the theatre. In 1892, Smythe Pigott expressed doubt whether 'in a country and community so saturated with politics as our own, the public would care to have places of amusement turned into political arenas'.[3] In 1909 his successor told the Parliamentary Joint Select Committee that

The stage is not a political arena, and it is not desirable that specially important political questions, perhaps involving diplomatic relations with Foreign Powers, should be touched upon.[4]

Apart from a general antipathy towards serious issues, a specific political bias was often perceived, and critics of censorship asserted that 'plays running counter to any governmental policy' were 'condemned from the very outset'.[5] In reviewing an anti-Soviet play in 1922, *The Observer* commented that 'A pro-Bolshevist play would have been interesting and difficult to write, but it might have had trouble with the Censor'.

The right of the Lord Chamberlain to censor plays derived from Robert Walpole's Licensing Act of 1737, which, however, had laid down no specific rules or guidance. The Theatres Act of 1843 confirmed and expanded his powers, specifying that he should refuse a licence whenever he was 'of opinion that it is fitting for the preservation of good manners, decorum or of the public peace so to do'.

The Case of 'The Russian Monk'

In 1909, the government responded to the increasing complaints of writers' by introducing a Joint Select Committee to investigate theatre censorship. This concluded by confirming the principle, and defining the boundaries more precisely.[6] One apparent loophole was that theatre clubs with private memberships were outside the Lord Chamberlain's power, but this probably served as a safety valve, helping to defuse confrontations, since the potential for an occasional Sunday performance to influence society was limited. As one manager observed, the clubs also operated self-censorship:

We are outside the Censor's jurisdiction here, and for that very reason we have to be careful of the plays we do. If it got about that we were using our privilege to do improper plays, our membership would go down immediately.[7]

One of the conscious motives behind the suppression of The Russian Monk in 1918 was the desire to forestall other plays on the same theme.[8] This highly fictionalized and jingoistic melodrama about the life of Rasputin has little theatrical merit, though the strong pro-British and anti-German messages might reasonably have been expected to please the British authorities: the play was certainly not intended to be politically subversive, and its rejection was ostensibly because its characters included the Russian Emperor and Empress.

But the issue was more complex than this, and the process of censorship did not begin with the Lord Chamberlain. In October 1917, four months before the play was submitted, Brigadier General G. K. Cockerill wrote to the Lord Chamberlain's office, stating that representatives of the Russian General Staff had informed him of plans to produce a play about Rasputin:

They have asked us to prevent its representation if possible, because it can only give offence to Russians. Would you be so very kind as to ask the officials who read plays for the Lord Chamberlain to look out for this play when it comes along, and could you arrange that it shall not be passed for representation unless it is innocuous from the point of view of our Allies?[9]

In reply, Sir Douglas Dawson promised that 'special attention' would be given to the play, and when The Russian Monk was submitted, the Lord Chamberlain warned the prospective manager that it was 'one which calls for special consideration'. He sent the script to the War Office, suggesting that the Russian General Staff should read and comment on it, though his letter makes clear that such a procedure was not officially recognized:

Kindly treat this matter as private and confidential as I have no right to part with the scrip [sic].[10]

He appended the comments of the two official readers, Ernest Bendall and G. S. Street, neither of whom had recommended it for licence. Bendall was greatly concerned about the implications of presenting an ineffective ruler to British audiences:

There is no intrinsic harm in this unpleasant farrago; but at this critical moment the personal introduction upon our stage of misguided Royalties like those of Russia (closely related as they are to our own King) seems most undesirable.[11]

Street took the same view, finding

something indecent in the exhibition of the weakness and misfortunes of the Russian Royalties so soon after their deposition.

He judged the play entirely from the perspective of the old Russian Order, assuming the irrelevance of the Bolsheviks: 'If there were any Russian Government with regular representatives they would be affronted. I do not think advantage should be taken of their non-existence.'[12]

Cockerill agreed that while there was no objection to the play 'on strictly military grounds', it should nevertheless be banned as 'objectionable'. Other members of the War Office contributed to the debate: one suggested that the problem could be alleviated by changing the names of the Czar and Rasputin, and introduced a revealing argument in favour of licensing:

Were it prohibited, certain people would be sure to say that attempts were being made to support and protect the late Czar . . . and this would be far more dangerous than any mischief that would result if no prohibition.[13]

But another official, evincing surprise that 'Sovereigns were allowed on the stage in such an unfavourable light', raised an important issue by asking 'If we pass this twaddle who will believe us if later we have to refuse something serious?'[14]

On 19 March, the Lord Chamberlain informed the author, Geo De Gray, that he was unable to grant a licence. DeGray was shocked, having already booked a tour and prepared the costumes and scenery, and volunteered to make any required alterations: the Lord Chamberlain explained that this would not be sufficient.

Over a year later, in July 1919, DeGray asked him to reconsider, but Street still insisted that to present the play 'would be an outrage on all decent feeling'. Bendall confirmed that

the objections to it retain their full force, and are beyond the possibility of removal by alteration.[15]

DeGray made one final, desperate, and abject attempt two years later, writing to the Lord Chamberlain on headed paper, and now listing *The Russian Monk* as one of his fourteen plays:

Now that the Political unrest with regard to Russia has subsided it occurred to me that The Lord Chamberlain might be prevailed upon to re-

consider his decision with regard to the above drama. . . . If you refer to the manuscript you will find that there is nothing of an offensively Political nature in it . . . and, of course, I would be only too happy to make any alterations or eliminations to 'characters' or 'Locale' which may be considered necessary.[16]

The Lord Chamberlain replied that he saw 'no reason for altering the decision' he had previously made.

The Russian Monk was a weak and poorly written play, but in deciding whether to license it no account was taken of its quality, its accuracy, or its sympathies. The only argument advanced in favour of licensing it was the highly political suggestion that to prohibit it might actually cause more trouble.

The censors – in this case the War Office and Russian staff officers as well as the Lord Chamberlain – were concerned to prevent a precedent, and took very seriously the dangers of portraying an incompetent ruler related to the British monarchy. When in 1928 a Russian play called *Rasputin* was submitted, it was therefore again rejected immediately, because of its portrayal of a weak Czar and a powerful and villainous Czarina:

The objection, I think fatal, is the presentation of the Czar and Czarina in the lights indicated above, whatever truth there may be in the picture. It would obviously be deeply offensive to the King.[17]

Never on 'Red Sunday'

In 1929, *Red Sunday* marked the first serious attempt by a British dramatist to chronicle the events surrounding the Russian Revolution.[18] Hubert Griffith's play had been directed by Komisarjevsky, with Robert Farquharson as Lenin and John Gielgud as Trotsky, and was submitted for licence to enable this private production to transfer to the West End.

Again, the question of censorship had been raised in advance. Following the restricted performance, *The Times* published an editorial under the heading 'A Dramatic Indiscretion', condemning the play for its sympathy towards the revolution and its criticisms of pre-revolutionary Russia. The newspaper was particularly disturbed that Griffith had dared to depict the Czar, Nicholas II, noting that 'the accuracy or inaccuracy is not for the moment in question'. Despite claiming that a general principle was at stake, the editorial disclosed that the issue was also very specific:

There must be many Russian exiles (and many English are profoundly in sympathy with them) to whom the Bolshevist rule represents the loss of nearly all, material and personal, that made life dear to them. . . . A dramatist is entitled to disagree with their politics, but not, in a public show, to assault their private memories.[19]

This article doubtless drew more attention to the play, and the Keeper Of The Privy Purse at Buckingham Palace sent a memorandum to the Lord Chamberlain reporting a complaint from Monsieur Bark, the former Russian Finance Minister, and now Managing Director of the Anglo-International Bank. Bark had told him that 'all persons of Russian nationality were very indignant' that such a play had been produced. Not satisfied by the explanation that the production was outside the Lord Chamberlain's jurisdiction, Bark had sought an assurance from Buckingham Palace that the play would not be performed again:

I promised to write to you and ask you whether some pressure could not be brought on the Manager of this theatre to discontinue a performance which was giving so much pain to Russians in London.[20]

The Lord Chamberlain replied that he fully understood the Russian unease, and that the King had already spoken to him about banning the play, following a protest by the Duchess Xenia. However, he had

explained to His Majesty that the play had not received a Licence, and that its performance was of a private character within the walls of a club in which I had no jurisdiction, nor would it be possible *or politic* [*my emphasis*] for there to be any official interference in plays so produced.[21]

Lord Cromer went on to suggest that the play was unlikely to be heard of again, but it was submitted for licence later that month, by a manager who expressed himself willing to remove the characters of the Czar, Czarina, and Czarevitch.

In his reader's report, Street admitted that *Red Sunday* was 'far better than other plays' about the Soviet Union, and that many of its details were factual: he commented that there was 'nothing in the play of the ordinary causes of banning'. But Cromer refused the licence, making no reference to the pressure which had already been put on him. Instead, he disingenuously claimed that decisions as to what could and could not be portrayed on stage must be 'governed by circumstances and public taste'. He also specified that the play was beyond altering for possible public performance:

I do not think it to be in keeping with the general trend of sympathies and feelings in this country to have such a play staged for public performance now or in the near future. It could not fail to cause resentment in the minds of too many people to show the tragedy of [the] Russian Revolution [which] has already meant great anguish and suffering.[22]

The text of *Red Sunday* was published with the words 'Banned by the Lord Chamberlain' on the cover, and Griffith wrote an introduction bitterly attacking censorship. Insisting that he had already imposed a considerable degree of self-censorship in his treatment of the Czar, and had 'strained every endeavour to make the portrait as sympathetic as was conceivably consistent with the truth', he was particularly incensed that no account was taken of historical accuracy:

The question of whether you had treated the facts fairly or unfairly, whether your account was impartial or prejudiced, biased or unbiased, was never for a moment under discussion. The Lord Chamberlain, when he gave you his most solemn assurance that he would not be able to licence [*sic*] the play, had not read a line of the play.[23]

Griffith argues that having created a picture of Lenin 'as a murderer, a maniac, a deluded fanatic', the establishment found a more accurate perspective to be unacceptable, and he identifies a concerted media conspiracy to prevent the publication of alternative views:

The play contained no new fact that was not well known to anyone who had read fifty pages of any official and impartial history. But it had come up against a certain side of British susceptibility. The truth – or even a part of the truth – must not be told on the stage.[24]

Silencing 'Roar China'

The last script which I wish to consider is a translation of Sergei Tretiakov's *Roar China*, which had already been performed in Germany, the Soviet Union, and the USA, and which was submitted for performance at the Festival Theatre, Cambridge, in May 1931.[25] The play was based on a real incident of 1926, in which British gunboats had threatened to destroy an entire Chinese town in revenge for a single British death, and was an indictment of British and American colonial imperialism, racism, and exploitation.

Gray had had many previous conflicts with the Lord Chamberlain, and his articles in the *Festival Theatre Review* chart the running battles which he fought over censorship. It was here, in February 1929, that he described his production of Ernst Toller's *Hoppla!* as having been 'mutilated' by censorship, and in 1927 the Lord Chamberlain excised in its entirety the one speech from an anti-Bolshevik melodrama which had been critical of the Russian aristocracy and the Czar.[26]

In submitting *Roar China*, Gray therefore anticipated difficulties and even opposition. Acknowledging that Tretiakov's play was full of anti-English propaganda, he compared producing it to 'holding a wasp up by its sting', arguing that the effect of seeing propaganda directed against one's own country could only be amusing. Then, in an attempt to pre-empt a possible banning, he added that if the Lord Chamberlain should make the mistake of taking the play seriously, 'history will have one of the best jokes against his department that it has yet had'.[27]

On reading the script, Street identified 'bias', but was not sure whether this was pro-'proletariat' and anti-capital and 'Imperialism', or pro-yellow and anti-white, but the former is the more probable and the play a piece of Soviet propaganda.

After listing some of the 'impossibly coarse passages' which would have to be changed or cut from any play, he moved on to his main complaint:

the play as a whole is obviously dubious in its bias against or libel on this country and the methods of its representatives. Our naval officers are stupidly brutal throughout.

However, Street wondered whether in spite of this, and given where it was to be performed, licensing the play might draw less attention to it:

My personal opinion is that as no harm could be done by its production in Cambridge, where no one could believe the picture, and as it is extremely unlikely to be done elsewhere, having no prospect of popularity and except for the Chinese local colour being uninteresting, the Festival Theatre might be allowed to do it with the necessary cuts.[28]

Lord Cromer was similarly undecided, sending the script to the Home Office with a confidential letter which echoes Street's suggestion, but expresses concern about 'Soviet propaganda':

I am always anxious, as far as possible, to cut political censorship out of the theatre, but in this particular play it seems to me very near the line.

Cromer suggests that while the play could be fictionalized by changing names and details, it would still be 'objectionable as regards a libel on this country'. He then tries to balance whether the repercussions will be more harmful if he passes or rejects the script:

There is little doubt that if this play is refused a Licence there would be the usual paragraphs in the papers, but if it were licensed we should certainly have further endeavours made for the production of Soviet Propaganda Plays, which I cannot help thinking the Government would consider most undesirable.[29]

The Home Office passed Cromer's letter and

the script to 'the Division here which deals with questions of Soviet Propaganda', which in turn passed it on to the Foreign Office.

Soliciting Outside Opinions

When the Foreign Office returned it, they enclosed a report by a British official who had seen the play in Frankfurt, and who described it as 'a peculiarly venomous piece of Bolshevist propaganda – directed chiefly against the British'. On that occasion it had been decided not to complain about the production

on the grounds that however unfair and detrimental to British prestige the play may be any such protest abroad would give it greater prominence and do more harm than good.[30]

The implication seemed to be that for similar reasons a licence could now be granted, but the Home Office suggested that Cromer consult the Admiralty. Cromer immediately sent the script to Rear-Admiral G. K. Chetwode, actively seeking support to refuse a licence:

I cannot but think that the Royal Navy, and indeed large sections of the British public and the Press, would strongly resent the presentation of a play which the British Consul-General at Frankfort [sic] stigmatizes as a peculiarly venomous piece of Bolchevist [sic] propaganda. I am therefore inclined to refuse a licence for the Play, as once it is licensed I cannot very well restrict it to performances at the Theatre at Cambridge.[31]

Chetwode replied very promptly, insisting that 'the whole Play must be regarded as Bolshevik and anti-Western civilization propaganda', and categorically insisting that it should not be performed:

I am authorized to inform you officially that the Admiralty strongly object to this play being licensed to Cambridge or anywhere else under British control. We consider it especially undesirable that young and inexperienced undergraduates should be subjected at their age to this kind of malicious anti-British propaganda.[32]

The licence was refused, and Roar China was never seen in Cambridge; however, a final episode in the saga occurred when, after a private performance in Manchester by the Unnamed Society, a member of the public complained to the Lord Chamberlain, insisting that 'The actors in it I know personally as "Reds".' A local review was enclosed which, under the headline 'Clever Drama, but Virulent', described the play as 'pure Soviet propaganda' and 'anti-British'.[33]

The Lord Chamberlain promptly contacted Salford's Chief Constable, asking him to find out whether the production had really been private, but the police took their enquiries further than this: not only were the society and its reputation investigated through a secret informant, but individual officers were personally identified and discussed. The assumptions and prejudices of the police are clear from their report, which reassures the Lord Chamberlain regarding the nature and class of those who belong to the society:

The membership is most select and includes a number of University Professors. . . . Admission to the Society is by invitation, and only persons of considerable ability and influence are approached.

The background of the members was seen as a guarantee of their decency, and the fact that they could not be Communists:

Any suggestion that the Society is a Communistic organization would appear to be wholly refuted by the influencial [sic] public positions and social standing of the majority of its members, and my informant assures me definitely that this is not the case. . . . I could find nothing that would support the suggestion that Soviet Propaganda had been the aim of the Society in this production.

However, because actors were sometimes imported from outside the society, it was

possible for a non-member holding communistic views to take part in the productions, although personally I am of the opinion that this is very improbable as every precaution is taken to prevent undesirables from entering the Society.[34]

The investigations went no further, but Roar China was not performed again. In 1936 the Manchester Repertory Theatre enquired about a possible production, but abandoned the idea when informed by the Lord Chamberlain that the play was unlicensed.

Licenser or Censor?

A recently published defence of censorship under the Lord Chamberlain insisted that he 'regarded himself as the licenser of plays rather than as a censor'. It is true that relatively few plays were categorically refused licences, but the real power of censorship is often insidious rather than conspicuous. Writers and managers knew the constraints within which they were expected to operate, and as the same account uncritically remarks, they 'were often able to adapt their work to meet the Lord Chamberlain's requirements'.[35] In 1934, Hubert Griffith lamented the

unborn children' – the plays that a generation of intelligent young dramatists might have liked to have written but had been warned that they must not write.[36]

It is impossible to measure accurately the significance of the Lord Chamberlain and his examiners in determining the political content of performed plays, but there are several lessons which can be drawn from the evidence of the plays discussed above. First, although nominally it was the Lord Chamberlain who made decisions about plays, scripts were unofficially passed to government ministries and beyond in order to solicit opinions. The Lord Chamberlain appears to have been ready to ban a play which caused concern to anyone whose opinion he thought important.

Second, 'truthfulness' in a play was largely irrelevant. Since the Lord Chamberlain and his readers believed that their own opinions were balanced, any plays which contradicted these views must demonstrate 'bias'. Sometimes the truth was too dangerous to acknowledge, as Hubert Griffith perceived:

The British Public must be maintained in its delusions, like a lunatic beyond hope of recovery, and shut away from its possibility of arriving one step nearer the truth.[37]

Third, the quality of a text was equally irrelevant. While there may be no inherent link between the politically and aesthetically progressive, both *Roar China* and *Red Sunday* could have introduced new forms to British theatre. The Lord Chamberlain's political sensitivities coincidentally hindered artistic developments.

Fourth, deliberate and probably successful attempts were made to discourage future plays about an unwelcome subject by preventing a precedent. No less significant is the agonizing over whether granting a licence to an unwelcome text might cause less controversy than refusing it.

However, perhaps the most remarkable point to emerge from all the evidence considered here is how seriously the issue of censorship was taken at the highest levels of government. Perhaps the playwrights would have been surprised to discover the dangers perceived in their work, and it is beyond the scope of this article to estimate whether the power and importance of the theatre were exaggerated.

The importance of political as opposed to religious and moral censorship by the Lord Chamberlain has often been understated. In this article I have concentrated on a few plays, and much more work remains to be done on the fascinating material which has at last become available. But it is clear that at least in its attitude to plays about the Soviet Union, the Establishment was unwilling to allow the theatre to raise political debate. The final word belongs to Hubert Griffith:

The Russian Revolution, in a sense, is historic. Were it completely so, had it been long petrified into history books, in the dead form of all finished and completed things, it would matter to no one – and could be performed on the stage with impunity. Because, however, its consequences are not yet exhausted, because its after-effects are still living, breathing realities, still an imminently near lesson to every civilized community (either in the sense of what to do, or what to avoid) – because, in a word, almost any aspect of this fantastically interesting phenomenon is of weight and importance and exactly the sort of thing that modern drama should make it its duty to deal with – therefore it must be snubbed officially and the right to perform it unconditionally withheld.[38]

Notes and References

1. Unsigned comment on the *The Russian Monk*, by Geo DeGray, in the Lord Chamberlain's files on Censorship. The play itself is in the Lord Chamberlain's Collection of Unlicensed Plays.

2. The best known is Richard Findlater's valuable *Banned! A Review of Theatrical Censorship in Britain 1901-1968*, and the most comprehensive and academic John A. Florance's *Theatrical Censorship in Britain 1901-1968*, unpublished Ph. D Thesis, University of Wales, 1980. John Johnston, a former member of the Lord Chamberlain's Office who has had prior access to many of the papers and much relevant information, has published *The Lord Chamberlain's Blue Pencil* (London, 1990).

3. E. F. Smythe Pigott, cited in James Woodfield, *English Theatre in Transition 1881-1914* (Beckenham, 1984), p. 113.

4. G. A. Redford, from *Report from the Joint Select Committee of the House of Lords and the House of Commons on the Stage Plays (Censorship), together with the Proceedings of the Committee, Minutes and Appendices* (H.M.S.O., 1909), cited in John A. Florance, op, cit., p. 259.

5. Dorothy Knowles, *The Censor, the Drama, and the Film 1900-1934* (London, 1934), p. 122.

6. The report was published on 11 November 1909, and consisted of 375 pages. Of the seven justifications for refusing a licence, three had direct political implications: a play must not 'represent on the stage in an invidious manner a living person, or any person recently dead'; it must not 'be calculated to impair friendly relations with any Foreign Power'; and it must not 'be calculated to cause a breach of the peace'. See *Report from the Joint Select Committee of the House of Lords and the House of Commons on the Stage Plays*, op. cit. However, no recommendations were binding since no legislation was introduced.

7. Quoted in Hubert Griffith's 'Introduction' to the published text of *Red Sunday* (London, 1929), p. xv-xvi.

8. *The Russian Monk* was received by the Lord Chamberlain's Office on 22 February 1918.

9. Lord Chamberlain's Files relating to the Censorship of Plays, *The Russian Monk*, letter from War Office to Colonel Sir Douglas Dawson, 10 Oct. 1917.

10. Ibid., letter from Dawson to Cockerill, 4 Mar. 1918.

11. Ibid., reader's comment from Ernest A. Bendall, 25 Feb. 1918.

12. Ibid., reader's comment from G. S. Street, n.d.

13. Ibid., reader's comment, illegible signature, n.d.

14. Ibid., reader's comment, illegible signature, 14 Mar. 1918.

15. Ibid., memorandum from Ernest A. Bendall, 15 July 1919.

16. Ibid., letter from Geo A. DeGray to Reader of Plays, 28 June 1921.

17. Lord Chamberlain's Files on Censorship, *Rasputin*.

18. It was produced at the Arts Theatre on Sunday 27 June 1929.

19. *The Times*, 1 July 1929, p. 15.

20. Lord Chamberlain's Files relating to the Censorship of Plays, *Red Sunday*, unsigned memorandum from Keeper of the Privy Purse, Buckingham Palace, to the Lord Chamberlain, 3 July 1929.

21. Ibid., letter from Cromer to Keeper of the Privy Purse, Buckingham Palace, 4 July 1929.

22. Ibid., addition in red ink to reader's report, refusing a licence, 30 July 1929.

23. Hubert Griffith, 'Introduction' to *Red Sunday*, op. cit., p. xiv.

24. Ibid., p. 5.

25. Translated by Barbara Nixon, *Roar China* was submitted on 8 April 1931 for performances in the week beginning 4 May.

26. *Red Nights of the Tcheka*.

27. 'The Season's Programme', *Festival Theatre Review*, IV, No. 72 (18 April 1931), p. 9.

28. Lord Chamberlain's Files relating to the Censorship of Plays, *Roar China*, reader's report, signed G. S. Street, 8 April 1931.

29. Ibid., letter from Lord Cromer to Mr. Harris, Home Office, 10 April 1931.

30. Ibid., letter from A. Willert, Foreign Office, to Home Office, 22 April 1931.

31. Ibid., letter from Cromer to Rear-Admiral G. K. Chetwode, CB, CBE, 25 April 1931.

32. Ibid., letter from George Chetwode, addressed 'My dear Lord Cromer', 27 April 1931.

33. The production took place in Manchester in November 1931.

34. Lord Chamberlain's Files relating to the Censorship of Plays, *Roar China*, report by Salford City Police on the Unnamed Society, 17 Nov. 1931.

35. John Johnston, *The Lord Chamberlain's Blue Pencil*, op. cit., p. 21.

36. Dorothy Knowles, op. cit., p. 4.

37. Hubert Griffith, 'Introduction' to *Red Sunday*, op. cit., p. x.

38. Ibid., p. viii.

Glenn Loney

A Theatre of Pre-Depression: Economics and Apathy in New York

In an article in NTQ22 (May 1990), Glenn Loney clarified, with special concern for a British readership, the many 'Factors in the Broadway Equation'. In NTQ 30 (May 1992), he took a closer look at the productions of the 1990-91 season, with its glut of musicals, from the lavish to the just plain lousy, economic 'single-person shows' – and the sometimes more challenging products of the off-Broadway and not-for-profit sectors. Here, he continues to trace the long decline of the 'fabulous invalid' through the season of 1991-92 – a season overshadowed by the death of Joe Papp, the mourning for a great showman mixed with concern for the future of his Public Theatre enterprises. The paucity of productions on Broadway – where, while one show could lose its backers four million dollars overnight, *Peter Pan* took American audiences happily back to the traditions of English pantomime – continued to contrast with signs of life elsewhere, and new productions marked milestone-anniversaries for La Mama and the Manhattan Theatre Club. Glenn Loney, is a widely published theatre writer and teacher based in New York.

AMERICA'S current theatre problems are less concerned with artistry than they are with economics. Even if the nation were not stalled in a recession, the costs of production and of theatre maintenance would continue to rise. The question is: how high can ticket prices soar before audiences give up on the commercial theatre – and even the non-profit sector? On Broadway, the current weekly running costs of productions, especially musicals, is so high that a show needs glowing reviews, enthusiastic word-of-mouth, and near-capacity houses to survive, let alone pay off its investors.

In *The Performing Arts: the Economic Dilemma*, a study for the Twentieth Century Fund in 1961, economists William G. Bowen and William G. Baumol pointed out the inevitable fact that it would always take four musicians to play a quartet in live performance, no matter what ingenious labour-saving and cost-cutting methods might be achieved in agriculture and industry. And, as artists' wage expectations rose, nudged along by inflation, the costs to consumers would increase, perhaps exponentially. Of course video and CD technology can do for the arts what robotization did for Toyota: but then it's no longer live performance.

For Bowen and Baumol, who had closely studied European models of government subsidy, this was surely the answer for the performing arts – not only for survival but also for the achievement of excellence. And it's long been clear to anyone who cares about the arts, especially the theatre, that the cost of just one Stealth bomber would be a major and much-needed transfusion into the slackening funding of the National Endowment for the Arts. But as the American economy slides from recession into depression – with national leaders terrified of uttering that depressing epithet – and the streets of most cities thronging with the homeless and jobless, it is highly unlikely that theatres, commercial or otherwise, will receive governmental largesse,

This situation is something you could write a play about – just as a number of dramas have recently joined *As Is* and *The Normal Heart* to protest or mourn the Aids crisis. The problem with such thesis plays, unfortunately, is that they need perhaps the gift of an Ibsen to rivet the attention of audiences already numbed by images of despair on TV newscasts.

Half way through the new Broadway season, with too many famous theatres dark, there are four British and four American musicals still running from previous years. The one new fall musical, long in gestation but very brief of life, *Nick and Nora*, opened after many delays, only to be trounced by the critics and close in a matter of days. Perhaps the Thin Man was never meant to sing – or, thanks to videotapes, memories of William Powell were too strong for Barry Bostwick to overcome.

Success, Failure – and Nostalgia

The only major fall success was the London production of Brian Friel's *Dancing at Lughnasa*, which elicited critical raves. Some, like me, thought the performances splendid but the play weak because of Friel's excessive use of narration. Israel Horowitz's *Park Your Car in Harvard Yard* was notable for the performances of Jason Robards as a dying old bachelor schoolteacher and Judith Ivey as an abused young widow who comes to be his housekeeper. It turns out that he had given her and her entire family failing or very low grades in school, and was also, for a time, her mother's lover. Before his death, they find grace, in the manner of *Educating Rita*. Were it not for the characters Robards and Ivey create on stage, those the playwright has imagined would be *un*credible. And Zoe Caldwell's sure directorial hand was in evidence.

Clearly, rising production costs are frightening would-be producers away from Broadway. *Nick and Nora* cost over four million dollars, a total loss. And, in a city where there are daily bankruptcies of smart shops and summary firings of executives and office staffs, people are increasingly wary of spending, especially on ephemeral entertainments – of which the Great White Way has had its share recently. Although André Heller's shows have enjoyed acclaim in Europe, his old-time variety performance *Wonderhouse* – which had some very good acts – was spurned by most critics, and hence by audiences also. *Catskills on Broadway* provided Borscht Belt comedians; the Moscow Circus came again to Radio City Music

Hall; and another Russian circus played briefly at the Gershwin.

Early in this century, New York still had Christmas pantomimes, an inheritance from London, but they soon died out. Now they seem to be reborn, with the second annual visit to Broadway of *Peter Pan*, the flying musical with Cathy Rigby. (I saw it also in Montgomery at holiday season, though with different sets and actors, at the Alabama Shakespeare Theatre.) And all over America now, regional theatres are trotting out their *Christmas Carols*, ballet companies their *Nutcrackers*, and opera ensembles their *Amahls* or *Hansel and Gretels*. Panto lives!

The Broadway Alliance, a new scheme to produce cheaply with low ticket prices, generated two shows last season, alike unsuccessful with critics and audiences, though *Our Country's Good* might have prospered in a smaller theatre off-Broadway. Undaunted, producers have a new show mounted under the same conditions, *Crazy He Calls Me*. Unfortunately, another play, *Crazy for You*, is also to open about the same time. If one of them gets good reviews, maybe the other may profit from the confusion of titles. Or both may die the death.

There has not been a season within recent memory when there were so few openings on Broadway, not even in the depths of the Great Depression. All is not lost, however, for gradually some institutional theatres are being invited under the Broadway umbrella, even though they are not-for-profit operations. At Lincoln Center, where the Vivian Beaumont is in danger of becoming the John Guare State Theatre, his *Six Degrees of Separation* has closed (after 40 previews and 201 performances) to make way for his *Four Baboons Adoring the Sun*. Guare's *House of Blue Leaves* also had a long run at the Beaumont, which originally was intended to be a repertory theatre, featuring not only new plays by various authors, but also ancient and modern classics. But even Joe Papp, during his adventurous tenure at the Beaumont, couldn't make it work.

Now, succeeding Greg Mosher, André Bishop, formerly the risk-taking chief of

Playwrights Horizons, is running the Lincoln Center operation, long spurned by Broadway, while Broadway actor-director Don Scardino has taken over Bishop's old post. Because the Beaumont's second stage, the Newhouse, is so small, occasionally smaller-scale productions are shown on Broadway at the Cort, which housed David Mamet's *Speed the Plough* and now shelters Richard Nelson's *Two Shakespearean Actors*, seen first in England. (Interesting that Nelson's *Some Americans Abroad*, Mamet's *Glengarry Glen Ross*, Jules Feiffer's *God Bless*, and Miller's *Ride Down Mount Morgan* all had to be shown initially in Britain.)

Broadway has long been indebted to Ted Mann's Circle in the Square, which moved midtown from Greenwich Village. This is its fortieth anniversary – something of a record for institutional theatres in New York, since either they or their overburdened artistic directors tend to burn themselves out after a decade. With George C. Scott in a revival of Paul Osborn's sentimental and schematic *On Borrowed Time*, it was definitely nostalgia-time at the Square.

Moving to Broadway from Tammany Hall, the Roundabout offered a respectably performed production of Harold Pinter's disreputables in *The Homecoming*, but the material seemed dated – though not in the same way as Osborn's of course. Lindsay Crouse was a good foil for Roy Dotrice's Max. This was followed by Dürrenmatt's *The Visit*, with Jane Alexander as the deadly Claire. Roundabout productions are always strong on the quality of sets and costumes, though the diet of classics sometimes suffers from miscasting or inadequate direction. But these seemed pitched to a level appropriate to Broadway now. And, at the new Criterion, the Roundabout doesn't have the financial problems regular Broadway shows do.

A newcomer to midtown was Tony Randall's National Actors Theatre, long a dream of this performer, who now calls himself 'Founder and Artistic Director'. Advance broadcast ads heralded casts of stars, including the dubious Rob Lowe, a film actor more noted for those videotapes he made with those girls in that hotel room.

None the less, the initial presentation, Arthur Miller's *The Crucible*, was an impressive revival. Because of its structure as a classic tragedy – with overtones of Shaw's *Saint Joan* – this play has a timeless resonance which *Death of a Salesman* increasingly seems to lack. Martin Sheen was a craggy, anti-heroic John Proctor, with Maryann Plunkett, admired in *Me and My Girl*, as a simple but powerful Elizabeth Proctor. Michael York, Fritz Weaver, and Martha Scott recreated Salem's witchhunts in a setting of tortured old trees designed by David Jenkins.

Farewells to Old Friends

Sad to say, but now the most memorable shows on Broadway are memorial services for the fallen. The one for Colleen Dewhurst in late September was, though tempered with sadness at the loss, a festival of joy and laughter, as friends such as José Quintero, Robert Whitehead, Maureen Stapleton, Edward Albee, and many others recalled her wonderful talent and great generosity. When Colleen Dewhurst stepped down from the presidency of Actors' Equity in May 1991, she wrote:

I am so proud to be a part of this profession to which we all have dedicated our lives. You have proven to me what I have always thought to be true: there is no place like the theatre. We reach an audience – and each other – in a one-on-one experience that is like no other. In some way, we have all made a difference and touched each others' lives both professionally and personally, in ways large and small, obvious and unnoticed.

Colleen Dewhurst was the Earth Mother she often played in Eugene O'Neill's dramas.

Another terrible loss, not only to New York's theatre but that of the nation – in the extent of his influence as a producer and theatre-passionist – was that of Joseph Papp, founder and director of the New York Shakespeare Festival, with its two homes, the Delacorte in Central Park and the Public Theatre in the Village. Tributes were printed and uttered everywhere, some of the most sincere from those with whom he had most argued and fought.

Joe Papp was a visionary and a fighter, which made it possible for him to achieve at least some of his visions. Infatuated with the genius of Shakespeare and the power of his plays, Papp fought Robert Moses to get free Shakespeare into Central Park, where it thrives every summer. He saved and restored the old Astor Library – near the site of the infamous Astor Place Riots, which grew out of the enmity of the two Shakespearean actors, Macready and Forrest – turning it into a home for all kinds of experiments in performance, with five or six arenas.

Not only did Papp give many kinds of native talents – directors, actors, dancers, musicians, composers, designers, playwrights, dramaturgs – their entries into the theatre, but he also invited foreign masters to show their abilities. From the Public, *Hair* moved to Broadway, though somewhat transformed by Tom O'Horgan, while *A Chorus Line* also transferred, to become Broadway's longest-running musical (with 6,137 performances), and an important source of subsidy for the Shakespeare Festival's more adventurous forays into the avant garde.

Ironically, Papp loved to direct, but that was the theatre task he did with the least panache. Now and then, he seemed to have engaged idiosyncratic or disorganized directors so he could quarrel with them and take over direction of a new play. He was a force of nature in his determination to achieve his goals and fund his theatre, but he also fought fiercely for others in and out of the theatre. When the NEA, prodded by Senator Jesse Helms and an addled Congress, set its 'obscenity' tests on grant-recipients, Joe Papp rejected a $373,000 grant which his theatres badly needed. Had Joseph Papp been running the NEA, things would look quite different now for the performing arts in America.

But his illness had been taking its toll in the past year, and events at the Public and in the Park lacked some of the vitality of previous seasons. Indeed, Shakespeare in the Park last summer looked like two different programmes folded into one. Because there is a large potential Hispanic audience in New York – and Spanish-speaking talents eager to entertain – Papp had created the Festival Latino. One of his notable imports for this was Caracas's Rajatabla (see NTQ7, August 1986), and this past summer they were back, this time in the Park with a challenging Venezuelan vision of *The Tempest*. Earlier, Brazil's Teatro do Ornitorrinco presented an astonishing *Midsummer Night's Dream*, whose nudity provided occasion for tabloid excitement and tut-tutting.

JoAnne Akalaitis is Papp's beleaguered successor. At first, he announced last season that there would be a quadriga of directors, but this he must have seen would lead to the disaster of government by committee. Understandably, feminists have hailed the emergence of both Akalaitis and Ann Bogart as directors of quite original gifts: but Akalaitis has never had to *manage* an operation as large, complicated, and diverse as the Public, nor to make the many kinds of artistic decisions which will surely be required. Her experience with the avant-garde Mabou Mines ensemble and her own novel stagings give few indications that she has the breadth of Papp's vision and interest in things theatrical. Her *Henry IV, Parts I and II* last season can best be described as bizarre. No one wants the Public to falter, however, so theatregoers are crossing fingers for its good health.

In the Non-Profit Sector

Even as the Los Angeles Theatre Center died after six valiant years in downtown LA – a victim of its environment and economics – other New York ensembles passed milestones of survival. Ellen Stewart's La Mama ETC celebrated its thirtieth anniversary, a wonder when so many much younger than La Mama have burned out. Among the celebratory productions was a revival of *Futz*, Rochelle Owens's drama of a man in love with his pig – 'but it's a *female* pig', Owens used to insist – and performance artist Ping Chong's twentieth-anniversary salute, *Dreaming in Public. Nosferatu, a Symphony of Darkness* was revived for the occasion, mingling Yuppies, Mexican *Muertos*, and the cast of the old vampire saga in very stylish, high-tech ways.

The return of *Nosferatu, a Symphony of Darkness*, for the thirtieth anniversary season at La Mama.
Photo: Carol Rosegg.

The Manhattan Theatre Club was twenty years old, and its slick production of Terrence McNally's Aids-related play, *Lips Together, Teeth Apart*, had an extended run in its main theatre, then moved to the Lucille Lortel Off-Broadway. Shirley Lauro's *A Piece of My Heart*, a series of short scenes on the disillusion of women nurses, entertainers, and Red Cross aides serving overseas, got a fast-moving production: but one only got snapshots rather than characters as a result.

The WPA Theatre was fifteen years old this season, but its production of *The White Rose*, dealing with the bravery of Sophie Scholl and her friends in opposing the Nazis in Munich in the Second World War, was dismissively received by the press. And John Houseman's Acting Company, usually on tour, was ten years old, as was the Vineyard Theatre, which specializes in music-theatre and poetic oddities.

Other interesting non-profit ensembles were between decades, variously struggling to survive. Under Tanya Berezin's artistic direction, the Circle Rep has taken a downward turn from its greater days under Marshall Mason, where it often had new plays by Lanford Wilson. Berezin announced early on that she was interested in dramas about the family and human relationships. Instead of revisiting King Lear and family, however, she has chosen a strange succession of views of society's walking-wounded, and *Babylon Gardens*, by Tim Mason, even with Timothy Hutton and Hector Estrada, was about as hopeless – even pointless – a picture of life in the big city as possible, the central figure being a drug-sotted anaesthetist.

The Good Times Are Killing Me used words and music to evoke the inevitable estrangement of a black girl and her white chum in an increasingly polarized racial milieu. Ultimately it wasn't more hopeful than Mason's play, but it was a lot more fun to watch. Produced by Second Stage, this moved to a commercial off-Broadway house, the Minetta Lane Theatre. The American Jewish Theatre features musicals with Jewish themes, so its revival of *Rags*, which had rapidly failed on Broadway despite Teresa Stratas as its star and Charles Strouse's attractive melodies, was welcome, though its revised book was still too complicated.

At the Astor Place Theatre, *The Radiant City* was a most unusual exploration of the career of Robert Moses in his efforts to affect the lives of New Yorkers through control of their highways and parks. The huge and miniscule puppets of Theodora Skipitares – with their amusing and very visible handlers – made this something special. It is festival-worthy, despite a deliberate amateurishness that is annoying.

The Pearl Company's *Tartuffe* in its tiny theatre was too small in every way, but that didn't deter the group from a season of Euripides, Ibsen, Shakespeare, and Chekhov. The Pan-Asian Repertory offered *The Dressing Room*, by Kunio Shimizu, an unusual drama-metaphor set in a room haunted by the unseen, unheard ghosts of women in the Japanese theatre of the past – when women were not permitted on stage. And at the Irish Arts Center, *Damien* was an affecting monodrama, though as the Leper Priest William Walsh should not have tried a Flemish accent.

Linda Pakri's Arts Club Theatre, in the social hall of Our Lady of Vilnius, specializes in plays from the Baltic nations. Matti Unt's *Doomsday* proved an interesting exposure of these sensibilities, while *Distant Fires*, by Kevin Heelan, by the Atlantic Theatre Company, was notable for the fact that the cast actually poured cement into flooring-forms on a high-rise in Maryland. Audience members who remembered *The Contractor* compared this activity with putting up the tent in David Storey's drama. Essentially about survivals of racist attitudes among working men, it was very well produced, if schematic in its discoveries.

But these are all from the non-profit sector – offering limited runs in usually small theatres, often remodelled churches. Commercial off-Broadway had some musical holdovers from last season, joined successfully by *Return to the Forbidden Planet* from London, but in a very small – even historic – venue which used to sport an old sign: 'Variety Photoplays'.

At the Orpheum, *Unidentified Human Remains and the True Nature of Love* explored serial murder, deviant sex, and other such modern problems in Edmonton, Ontario. Critical response to Brad Fraser's darkly amusing play was cold, but the production was dynamic and engaging. At the Lamb's Theatre, *Beau Jest* imagined a Jewish career girl falling in love with the escort she'd hired to act as a fiancé to please her parents. The problem: he's a goy. James Sherman's boulevard farce has a future in stock.

Jane Anderson's *The Baby Dance*, at the Lortel, was an unsatisfactorily resolved study of a barren couple paying for a surrogate mother, only to find her child is defective. Anderson's interest in such concerns, as in her drama about the homeless, *Food and Shelter*, is commendable, but both seem better suited to film.

Something new and strange in dinner-theatre is *Song of Singapore*. The amazing designer John Lee Beatty has taken an old second-story ballroom near Union Square and turned it into a glitzy-sleazy Chinese nightclub in Singapore just before the invasion of the Japanese. The audience, who can buy Thai food or drinks (such as the Frank Sumatra, the Taiwanon, or the Shirley Temple of Doom), are involved in the club's entertainment and a mystery-drama with stolen treasure as well.

Much more high-minded is En Garde Arts, which draws attention to interesting problems and places with site-specific productions. *Another Person Is a Foreign Country* was presented in the ruins of The Towers, a noble castellated nursing-home on Upper Central Park West. Almost a homage to Robert Wilson, this avant-gardist staging, directed by Anne Bogart, involved a number of disabled performers.

The increasing attractions of dance and music theatre. Top: the American Indian Dance Theatre in its production of *Eagle Dance*, during its season at the Joyce (photo: Don Purdue). Bottom: the Pina Bausch Tanztheater, Wuppertal, in its production of *Bandoneon* during its season at the Brooklyn Academy of Music (photo: Detlef Erler).

Those New Yorkers who really enjoy theatre, but on big stages in impressive productions, are increasingly attracted to dance and music theatre. Among the most attractive of such offerings was Hanay Geiogamah's American Indian Dance Theatre at the Joyce. Geiogamah is first a playwright on Indian themes, but he has found that native American dances – theatricalized, of course – are more interesting to a general audience. The ensemble dance in fantastic costumes with mystery and vigour.

Pina Bausch brought her Tanztheater from Wuppertal to the Brooklyn Academy, with two typically minimalist works for dance purists. The paucity of actual dance in *Bandoneon* was exasperating, but the way Bausch encourages her dancers to function as performance-artists, and the way they are orchestrated in the often haunting milieus, suggests Robert Wilson's influence, though Bausch is very much an original. *Carmen Miranda*, an evocation of the Brazilian cinema star, also played at BAM, while the world of Ruth St. Denis and of Ted Shawn's 1920s modern dances was recreated at Danspace by the Denishawn Repertory Dancers. A marvel to see – and a strong contrast to the often opaque performance art of Decodanz and Koppelvision, whose images are none the less often astonishing.

But if you are a lover of the American musical, it's no longer to Broadway that you turn. Frank Loesser's *The Most Happy Fella* had an expansive revival at Lincoln Center by the New York City Opera. And this was in rep, in a season which ended mid-fall: so it's perhaps overkill that the musical is also opening at the intimate midtown Booth Theatre, imported from the historic Goodspeed Opera House in Connecticut. This is a much smaller-scale production, and the musical of necessity plays differently in a small house.

One hopes the City Opera will bring their *Fella* back as well when their summer season begins: but the company's director, Christopher Keene, has indicated he's not enthusiastic about programming musicals unless they have operatic qualities. The revival of *Brigadoon* found a welcoming public, but if such shows cannot be kept alive in repertory, what will become of this American theatrical heritage?

As with the English National Opera and Covent Garden, the City Opera has always been more adventurous than the Met. This season among the eminently theatrical productions have been a new 'dance-opera', *The Mother of Three Sons*, drawing on African tales and big-city realities, and conceived by Bill T. Jones; Korngold's *The Dead City*, a revival with marvellously evocative still and moving projections of historic Bruges; Bernd Alois Zimmerman's savage *Die Soldaten*, musically and technically fiendishly difficult to stage; and even theatrically interesting productions of those old warhorses, *Cav and Pag* and *Traviata*.

Both houses are sold out these days, in part because there are no new spectacles on Broadway. *The Death of Klinghoffer* packed them in at the Brooklyn Academy of Music, even with Alice Goodman's controversial libretto and John Adams's now-less-than-minimalist music.

But the trophy for spectaculars goes to the Met. With a stunning *Fanciulla del West*, conceived in a style of romantic realism worthy of David Belasco, the play's original author and director, Puccini himself was challenged by the vitality of the production, complete with knockout bar-room brawl. And even this was soon eclipsed by the last hurrah of the Mozart Year, John Corigliano's *The Ghosts of Versailles*. Librettist William Hoffman and the composer imagined the ghost of Beaumarchais trying to save the ghost of his beloved Marie Antoinette from the guillotine, with the characters of *La Mère coupable* – Figaro and the Almavivas – absurdly involved. Meta-music theatre indeed!

Tony Pearson

Meyerhold and Evreinov: 'Originals' at Each Other's Expense

Our occasional series of original theatre documents continues with this translation, the first in English, of an article written in 1915 by the Russian director Nikolai Evreinov attacking his contemporary and erstwhile colleague Vsevolod Meyerhold for artistic plagiarism – an attack which, of course, reveals as much about the susceptibilities and private jealousies of its perpetrator as it does about its object. Tony Pearson, who currently teaches in the Department of Theatre, Film, and Television Studies in the University of Glasgow, accompanies his translation with a full introduction and commentary, setting the polemics within the context of the Russian and early Soviet theatre, and the subsequent, separate careers of the two personalities involved.

VSEVOLOD MEYERHOLD and Nikolai Evreinov, illustrious competitors in the early twentieth-century Russian theatre, were never on good personal or professional terms. Indeed, their deep mutual dislike fuelled an enduring rivalry in which each compulsively sought to eclipse the other in terms of originality and reputation. They would periodically engage in unpleasant public polemics, accusing each other in print of aesthetic superficiality or the unacknowledged appropriation of directorial ideas. But the most bitter disagreement between them arose in 1915 when Evreinov vociferously complained that Meyerhold had stolen aesthetic concepts directly from him and used them shamelessly in his famous 1910 production of Molière's *Don Juan*.

Meyerhold – helped not least by his dominant involvement in the revolutionary avant-garde after 1917 – now possesses the sounder reputation and has attracted more scholarly attention. But there is plenty of evidence that Evreinov's comparative contribution to world theatre, too long regarded as peripheral, merits wider acclaim than it has usually been accorded.

Although they reached their positions in the vanguard of Russian modernism by vastly different routes, and were frequently at odds on aesthetic questions, Meyerhold and Evreinov had, at least in the pre-revolutionary phase, a number of characteristics in common. Both attracted notoriety, courted controversy, and developed a taste for self-promotion; both displayed an intellectual certainty often mistaken for arrogance; both practised a marked theatrical eclecticism which sometimes obscured their clarity of purpose; and both were at pains to represent themselves as the undisputed *originators* of their directorial concepts, even on occasions where such claims were somewhat dubious or debatable.

They shared a pathological contempt for stage naturalism – especially that of the Stanislavsky school – and a crusading belief in the re-integration of stage and audience through an appeal to the styles and conventions of earlier theatrical epochs. Each came to advocate the absolute centrality to modern theatre practice of expressive, metatheatrical strategies: *theatricality* in the case of Evreinov, *stylization* in the case of Meyerhold. In this belief, despite some differences of emphasis, the two were broadly in agreement: but there the similarities end. Meyerhold went on to prominence in the Soviet Constructivist theatre, while Evreinov, after his emigration from the Soviet Union in 1925, suffered a relative and permanent loss of influence.

The mutual antipathy between Meyerhold and Evreinov probably began to develop in 1908, when Vera Kommissar-zhevskaya dismissed Meyerhold from the post of artistic director of her prestigious experimental theatre and replaced him with the younger and considerably less experienced Evreinov. The latter had won Kommissarzhevskaya's admiration as a result of the notable success of his *Ancient Theatre* venture of 1907-08: the purpose of this had been a scholarly and detailed reconstruction of medieval theatre practice – and, significantly, it had given rise to Evreinov's claim to have originated 'the artistic-reconstructive method'.

For Kommissarzhevskaya, Evreinov's subtle aestheticism and sympathetic attention to the art of the actor contrasted sharply with Meyerhold's innovative fervour and dehumanizing, 'marionette-style', director-centred approach. Evreinov's comparatively successful (albeit brief) tenure of Meyerhold's old job probably contributed to a general souring of relations, but a climate of resentment and disregard between the two men was inevitable anyway, given their conflicting personalities and the uncompromising desire of each for critical supremacy over the other.

'Theatricality' and 'Stylization'

Evreinov, in particular, was unusually obsessive about receiving proper recognition for the formal invention of his dramaturgy, his theorizing of *theatricality*, and his production concepts. A number of sanctimonious protests about plagiarism are to be found in his writings, testifying to a biography of sensitivity about the ownership of intellectual property. Indeed, there were two notable instances – involving controversial disputes with former collaborators N. V. Driezen (on *Ancient Theatre*) and A. R. Kugel (on *Crooked Mirror Theatre*) – when Evreinov, at pains to establish his authorial rights, sought to characterize himself as a kind of 'Mozart' to his adversary's 'Salieri'.[1]

Thus, when the alleged plagiarist was Evreinov's true nemesis, Meyerhold, the infraction was perceived as all the more heinous, and Evreinov's desire for public recompense became all the more compulsive. A crucial and persistent preoccupation of Evreinov was that he and he alone (and certainly *not* Meyerhold of all people) should receive original credit for advocating the essence of the theory of *theatricality* which he claimed to have first articulated in his inaugural address to Kommissarzhevskaya's company in August 1908, published a few days afterwards as his article 'An Apologia for Theatricality'.

Evreinov was later fond of pointing out that Meyerhold, prior to the 'Apologia's' appearance, had still to make the conceptual shift from a *literary* to a truly stylized theatre, as evidenced by Meyerhold's insistence in an article published in 1908 that 'the growth of the New Theatre is rooted in literature . . . the theatre is prompted by literature'.[2] Only after the 'Apologia' had appeared did Meyerhold, according to Evreinov, begin to extol the virtues of *theatricality*, and especially of commedia dell'arte, asserting (but not in print until his 1912 article 'Balagan') that 'in order to save the Russian theatre from becoming the servant of literature, it is essential to return to the stage the cult of *cabotinage*'.[3]

Evreinov claims offence at such an apparently sudden change of theoretical direction, deploring the fact that Meyerhold subsequently pursued unambiguously theatricalist principles, without acknowledging their source, in a whole series of productions. This reaction of Evreinov's is, to say the least, uncharitable and disingenuous, founded on a purely selective reading of Meyerhold. Meyerhold's stance on literary-based theatre was by no means incompatible with stylization, and the bulk of the article from which Evreinov quoted makes this abundantly clear.

Meyerhold could reasonably have argued that he had in effect been espousing the cause of *theatricality*, in the more general sense of an anti-naturalistic *stylization*, since his inconclusive experimentation at the Moscow Art Theatre Studio back in 1905, and also in his subsequent productions of Maeterlinck's *Sister Beatrice* and of Blok's *Balaganchik*, both for Kommissarzhevskaya in 1906. Meyerhold could further have pleaded that his advocacy of a *stylized theatre*, following Vyacheslav Ivanov's 1902 call 'for the calculated stylization of the theatre of antiquity to replace the irrelevant truth of the modern stage', first appeared at much the same time as Evreinov's 'Apologia' in 1908, and was therefore decidedly not in arrears.[4]

However, as the text of the article reproduced below confirms, the dispute over whether Evreinov or Meyerhold first articulated and implemented the theatricalist principle of appeal to 'the theatre of antiquity' was to become even more vitriolic.

Someone Else's Originality?

Evreinov probably intended a severe snub to Meyerhold by omitting any reference to him in his hugely successful 1912 satire at Petersburg's Crooked Mirror Theatre based on Gogol's *The Government Inspector*. In this production, Evreinov staged the same two scenes from Gogol as parodies of five distinctive production styles – classical Russian melodrama, Stanislavsky, Max Reinhardt, Edward Gordon Craig, and the silent cinema. While Meyerhold might have been glad to be spared parodic scrutiny, the omission altogether from the production of a Meyerhold 'style' would have smacked of 'a judgement on Meyerhold's relative lack of importance among these other innovators'.[5]

Evreinov had earlier baited Meyerhold in his 'Apologia', and would do so again in the preface to his anthology *The Theatre as Such* (1913). But in 1915 came one of the most blistering public attacks that one artist can ever have made upon another. In the very first issue of Petrograd's *Journal of Journals*, Evreinov published his highly polemical 'Originality at Someone Else's Expense', which appears here in translation for the very first time. Indeed, this polemic has only once before (to this writer's knowledge) been cited, but never discussed in detail, in any critical writing on Evreinov.[6]

The reason, aside from the text's extreme rarity outside Soviet archives, may have something to do with its extravagance,

The antagonists in caricature. Top: Evreinov, as seen by M. P. Bobyshev: the ironic Latin legend reads, 'Nikolaus Evreinovius, Greatest of Innovators'. Evreinov's most hostile critic, G. K. Kryzhitskii, described it in 1928 as a 'semi-nude androgynous figure, a Raphaelite profile, holding a kind of "shameless", "voluptuous" lily'. Bottom: N. Ulyanov's caricature of Meyerhold in his own production of Blok's commedia playlet *Balaganchik* (1906) at the theatre of Vera Kommissarzhevskaya, St. Petersburg.

Yu Yur'ev in the title-role of Meyerhold's Don Juan.

egotism, hyperbole, and intemperance – all of which may incline the reader to dismiss it as excessive or dilettante. It amounts to a savage, outraged attack on Meyerhold for his alleged plagiarism of Evreinov. Composed in Evreinov's characteristically elevated style and shot through with conceited intellectualism and barbed sarcasm, it seeks retrospectively to discredit as derivative Meyerhold's famous 1910 production of *Don Juan*, and the subsequent programme of actor training at the Meyerhold Studio, alleging Meyerhold's appropriation of the 'artistic-reconstructive method' employed in Evreinov's *Ancient Theatre* productions of 1907-08 and 1911-12.

All the many italics, quotation marks, exclamations, proverbs, parentheses and ellipses of Evreinov's original have been preserved in the translation since, as well as being integral to the polemic, they help to convey an impression of the self-proclaimed

'original' who dared to lay such serious charges against the most widely recognized innovator of the day.

Although Evreinov's allegations in 'Originality at Someone Else's Expense' are extreme, they are probably not entirely without foundation: the eclectic Meyerhold was never averse to widespread cultural borrowings – a policy totally consistent with the aesthetic of modernism. Moreover, Meyerhold held strong views about his own status as 'author of the spectacle' even where an established, or even classical, script authored by another provided the theatrical pretext. He could quite reasonably have been creatively influenced by Evreinov's *Ancient Theatre* without plagiarizing its principles, in which case Evreinov might have been flattered rather than outraged by the attention.

But Evreinov, who was undoubtedly envious of Meyerhold's greater reputation, and probably also the glittering success of his *Don Juan*, was particularly incensed by the lack of any acknowledgement of his self-proclaimed 'artistic-reconstructive method'. Whether its use can be unambiguously ascribed to *Don Juan* is difficult to assess. In any event, the principles of *theatricality* or *stylization* were nobody's exclusive property: they were very much in the air around 1908, not only in Russia but in the European theatre generally. The fact that the Russian theatre at that time was supposed to be experiencing a 'crisis' encouraged Meyerhold, Evreinov, and other non-naturalist practitioners to compete for the role of its saviour.

Meyerhold Retaliates

Though Evreinov would not have known it at the time, Meyerhold for his part had already condemned Evreinov – for precisely the same crime of plagiarism – in a much earlier private letter which suggests that Evreinov was not the only one to be fiercely protective of his artistic plans and ideas. Replying on 30 July 1908 to a letter from

continued on page 330

Nikolai Evreinov

Originality at Someone Else's Expense

The longer I follow the activity of V. E. Meyerhold, the more I am astounded at the derivative nature of his talent. *'Je prend mon bien, où je le trouve'*,[1] said the genial Molière, obviously without realizing what temptation such words plant in the souls of all those who are quick to spot anything lying around just waiting to be picked up while its owner isn't looking. And Molière has finally discovered a truly 'original' imitator in the person of V. E. Meyerhold!

Now, after Siegfried Jakobsohn's substantial monograph on Max Reinhardt,[2] everyone can instantly perceive, from a cursory survey merely of the illustrations and the chronological list of that director's productions, the *derivation* (to put it mildly) of Meyerhold's so-called innovations from those of Reinhardt; especially if the reader still remembers that V. E. Meyerhold, having seen enough novelties in his time at the Berlin Kammerspiel, even 'sinned', under the immediate impact it made, by writing an unfavourable review in *The Scales* of Max Reinhardt's production of Maeterlinck's *Pelléas and Mélisande*, inadvertently revealing in the process his own abiding interest in his celebrated *stylization*.[3]

Having spluttered, not entirely successfully, about this 'Berlin stylization' ('the monkey, fondling the child, tortured it to death' – says the fabulist),[4] V. E. Meyerhold naturally rejoiced at the emergence of the *artistic-reconstructive method* of the 'Ancient Theatre', founded and initiated by me.[5] Of course, this gave the 'innovator', of whom the public had grown sick and tired,[6] the agreeable opportunity of changing 'his course',[7] without risk of apostasy.

Notes to the Translation

1. *'I take my material from wherever I find it.'* Evreinov's use of French is ungrammatical, since 'je prends' is preferred to his 'je prend'. It could simply be a misprint, but a subsequent error in Evreinov's use of Latin (see Note 22 below) may suggest more about his linguistic pretensions than his grammatical accuracy.

2. Siegfried Jacobsohn wrote at least *three* books on Reinhardt, but the source cited here must be his *Max Reinhardt* (Berlin, 1910).

3. This review by Meyerhold was first published in *Vesy* (*The Scales*), Moscow, 1907, p. 93-8, under the title 'Iz Pisem o Teatre: Berliner Kammerspiel, Regie Max Reinhardt' ('From Letters on the Theatre: the Berlin Kammerspiel, Director Max Reinhardt'). It subsequently appeared in Meyerhold's anthology *O Teatre* (*On Theatre*, 1912), and was later reprinted in V. E. Meyerhold, *Stati, Pis'ma, Rechi, Besedy* (*Articles, Letters, Speeches, Conversations*), Part 1 (Moscow, 1968), p. 162-6, under the title 'Max Reinhardt (Berliner Kammerspiele)'. Meyerhold had seen Reinhardt's productions on a visit to Berlin in April 1907.

4. Evreinov displays a typically Russian fondness for proverbs but is often guilty, as here, of straining his intended irony to the point where his meaning is rendered ambiguous.

5. The Ancient Theatre (Starinnyi Teatr), also referred to as 'The Theatre of Yore', was an ambitious undertaking that had a significant influence on the development of the pre-revolutionary Russian stage. Organized principally by Evreinov in association with a wealthy patron, Baron N. V. Driezen, it operated to critical acclaim in St. Petersburg and Moscow for two theatrical seasons, 1907-08 (for the Medieval Cycle) and 1911-12 (for the Spanish Cycle). It involved elaborate historical reconstructions, firstly of medieval moralities, folk plays, and farces, and later of the Spanish Golden Age dramas of Tirso de Molina, Lope de Vega, and Cervantes.

'Theatricality' was Evreinov's governing theoretical principle – equally applicable to art *and* life – to which he remained faithful throughout his long career. As early as 1908 he had published his seminal 'Apologia for Theatricality' ('Apologiya Teatral'nosti'), a powerful polemic in favour of the *conventional* (*uslovnyi*) nature of theatrical art, wherein anti-illusionist, expressive techniques confer an interpretive responsibility upon an active spectator inscribed as co-creator of the spectacle. Although Evreinov was not the only opponent at the time of psychological naturalism (Bryusov, Blok, and Meyerhold are among the others), he theorized against it more insistently, methodically, and obsessively than any of his contemporaries, placing emphasis upon *theatricality* as a theoretical system.

The Ancient Theatre introduced what Evreinov called his '*artistic-reconstructive method*', which envisaged not so much an archeological or antiquarianist directorial policy (as its title might suggest), but rather a creative, pragmatic retrospective – a 'free composition' – in the *spirit* and *style* of the original. Significantly, as well as reconstructing sets, costumes, acting styles, and so on, it set out to rediscover and

Sketch by Alexander Golovin of one of the backdrops for Meyerhold's 1910 production of Molière's *Don Juan* at the Alexandrinsky Theatre, St. Petersburg.

And that's how it turned out.

V. E. Meyerhold (bless him) fervently welcomed the appearance of my Ancient Theatre. True, just as before in respect of the theatre of Max Reinhardt, so now with regard to the Ancient Theatre, he again 'sinned'[8] (and how!) by penning an unfavourable review; nevertheless, whatever way you look at it, he greeted *my* method, became interested in it and even let the cat out of the bag by committing his so-called innermost thoughts to the pen.

Judge for yourselves!

'Taking account of the inclination of certain of today's theatres towards cheap modernism' – thus wrote this 'latter-day Molière'[9] in his book *On Theatre* (see the article 'The Ancient Theatre in Petersburg')[10] – 'and given the absence of any traditions at all in those theatres which are keeping a respectful distance away from the newest trends, there has arisen *at just the right time* [*my italics*] a theatre, which has set itself up to revive the creative powers of contemporary theatres by means of models of the uttermost simplicity and naivety from the ancient stage.' And, moreover: 'the theatre whose productions are strictly subordinated to the devices of traditional theatres can have a beneficial effect on the techniques of other theatres, even in the case where the latter do not include in their repertoire any plays from the theatre of olden times.'

This 'beneficial effect' V. E. Meyerhold certainly put to the test, first of all on himself, when he put on Molière's *Don Juan* at the Alexandrinsky Theatre in an approximation to the method of the Ancient Theatre which was plainly visible as such to everyone.[11]

The first step is always the hardest.

Developing a taste for what is *exclusively my* artistic-reconstructive method, V. E. Meyerhold, who simply could not accept the fact that the laurels had gone to the Ancient Theatre, intended to win back those laurels at whatever cost.

Having learned from the newspapers that the organizers of the Ancient Theatre intended to dedicate the next cycle of performances after the Spanish cycle to the Italian commedia dell'arte, V. E. Meyerhold decided on this occasion *to get in a pre-emptive strike*, come what may.

I say 'on this occasion' because there had already been one attempt on the part of this 'new Themistocles' to dispute the Ancient Theatre's claim to anteriority. This had occurred not very long before the realization of the Spanish cycle of the Ancient Theatre, when I was seriously alarmed by remarks in the press, in which V. E. Meyerhold explicitly 'threatened' to replicate as nearly as possible the celebratory and participatory *spectating conditions* of the chosen period.

A third and final season of the Ancient Theatre – focusing upon the commedia dell'arte – was planned for 1914-15, but never materialized due to the outbreak of war (see Note 25 below). For more information on the Ancient Theatre and on Evreinov's ideas on *theatricality* generally, see Tony Pearson, 'Evreinov and Pirandello: Twin Apostles of Theatricality', *Theatre Research International*, XII, No. 2 (1987), p. 155-6; Spencer Golub, *Evreinov: the Theatre of Paradox and Transformation* (Michigan, 1984), p. 107-43; and C. Moody, 'The Ancient Theatre in St. Petersburg and Moscow 1907-08 and 1911-12', *New Zealand Slavonic Journal*, No. 2 (1976).

6. Evreinov is tauntingly referring to Meyerhold's brief and controversial spell as artistic director at the theatre of actress-manageress Vera Kommissarzhevskaya in 1906-07. Kommissarzhevskaya, unable to endure Meyerhold's innovative excesses, which she felt reduced the actor to a mere puppet, shortly replaced him with Evreinov, after admiring the latter's work at the Ancient Theatre. The origins of the antipathy between the two men are probably traceable to this moment.

7. This is undoubtedly a general interpretation of Meyerhold's eclecticism as fickleness, but it may also be a more specific reference to what Evreinov somewhat selectively regarded as Meyerhold's indecent shift around 1908 from an entrenched notion of *literature* as the primary element of theatrical art to the advocacy of 'stylized theatre'.

8. Evreinov is suggesting that it is both offensive and hypocritical of Meyerhold to write unfavourable reviews and subsequently to appropriate the very ideas he was criticizing.

9. A rather cheap jibe, referring back to the opening quotation and identifying Meyerhold as an opportunist in the same mould as Molière, who, it seems, freely admitted his plagiarism. Evreinov probably intends the added irony that Meyerhold's 1910 production of *Don Juan* was as much an 'appropriation' of Molière as it was of Evreinov.

10. Evreinov here quotes verbatim from the opening paragraph of Meyerhold's review article 'Starinnyi Teatr v S.-Peterburge, pervyi period' ('The Ancient Theatre in St. Petersburg: First Period'), written in 1908 and first published in Meyerhold's anthology *O Teatre* (*On Theatre*, 1912). It was subsequently reprinted in V. E. Meyerhold, *Stati, Pis'ma, Rechi, Besedy*, Part 1, op. cit., p. 189-91, and is summarized in Edward Braun, *The Theatre of Meyerhold*, 1979, p. 101. Evreinov carefully omits the more critical sections of Meyerhold's review, which essentially argue that the Ancient Theatre 'fell between two stools' because it chose neither of the two obvious paths open to it.

It could, Meyerhold asserts, have approached the staging of ancient plays either *via* a precise archeological reconstruction, or by taking plays written *in the manner of* the ancient theatres and staging them as 'a free composition on the theme of the primitive theatre' – like Meyerhold's own production of Maeterlinck's *Sister Beatrice* at the theatre of Vera Kommissarzhevskaya in 1906. The Ancient Theatre,

according to Meyerhold, did neither: instead it took original texts and *stylized* them as free compositions resulting – for Meyerhold at least – in pastiche or parody. At issue here, therefore, is a conceptual difference between the two men with regard to the practical investigation of theatres of the past: but it is rather a narrow and pedantic one. Evreinov disingenuously chooses to play down this difference.

Meyerhold's claims for his own *Sister Beatrice* as a prior example of the reconstructive method are not without substance. One critic consistently hostile to Evreinov on both a personal and professional level later credited Meyerhold, and not Evreinov, with having pioneered the method with this particular production: see G. K. Kryzhitskii, *Rezhisserskie Portrety* (*Portraits of Directors*, 1928). This is probably a moot point, given the similarities and differences of approach. Both men were concerned with an idea, very topical at the time, which was also advocated by the likes of Vyacheslav Ivanov, Georg Fuchs, and Max Reinhardt. It is doubtful, however, whether anyone other than Evreinov would have gone to the trouble of trying virtually to patent the idea!

11. Meyerhold's production of *Don Juan* opened at the Alexandrinsky Theatre, St. Petersburg, on 9 November 1910, three seasons after the Ancient Theatre's Medieval Cycle. Purely because the production was based on the principle of scenic reconstruction invoking commedia dell'arte, Evreinov here attacks it for plagiarizing his Ancient Theatre. There are, however, some fundamental differences of approach that make this claim hard to sustain. In particular, Meyerhold was not aiming for the same overall effect as the Ancient Theatre. He was concerned to reconstruct *the production style of Molière's day* – the trappings of the court of Louis XIV – rather than the detail of the period from which the Don Juan myth derives (i.e., the time and place depicted in the play), while Evreinov preferred a more synthetic approach. However, by the time he wrote his article 'K Postanovke *Don Zhuana* Mol'era' ('Towards the Production of Molière's *Don Juan*', 1910), which first appeared in his anthology *On Theatre* (1912), Meyerhold seems to have further developed his views on historical reconstructivism, bringing them, in fact, closer to those of Evreinov. This is all the more reason why Evreinov's charges of artistic appropriation seem to be so exaggerated and misplaced.

Prior to *Don Juan*, Meyerhold had furthered his own reconstructive experiments in his production of Wagner's *Tristan and Isolde* for the Imperial Mariinskii Theatre in 1909, and also in his production of Calderon's *La Devocion de la Cruz*, which opened at Vyacheslav Ivanov's private Tower Theatre on 19 April 1910 – the latter showing an interest in Calderon and the Spanish Golden Age which predates Evreinov's.

12. Meyerhold, in common with many other contemporary artists, had long expressed a genuine interest in the expressive nature of both the Spanish Golden Age and the Italian commedia dell'arte. He had, for instance, begun to explore the conventions of commedia as early as his 1906 production of Blok's *Balaganchik* (*The Fairground Booth*, sometimes known as *The Puppet Show*), and again in Solovyov's

pre-empt the Ancient Theatre by announcing the commissioning of a translation of a Tirso de Molina play from the poet Piast, and the fact that he himself, entirely preoccupied with Spanish dramatists, was already organizing a circle of those interested in the Spanish theatre, and so on.[12]

Alas, the distinctly *'pre-emptive'* director turned out on this occasion to have been pipped at the post. And what happened? Did V. E. Meyerhold subsequently get to continue his work on a production of Tirso de Molina, with whom, according to his newspaper interviews, he was so fascinated? Not a bit of it. Tirso de Molina, as we predicted, was important to V. E. Meyerhold solely because V. E. Meyerhold wanted to pre-empt the Ancient Theatre's production of his play, *Marta la Piedosa*.[13] V. E. Meyerhold ceased to be interested in the work the instant it stopped serving as a springboard for his dubious reputation for 'originality'.

It happened differently with the commedia dell'arte, performances of which had been under preparation for three years by the organizers of the Ancient Theatre and which were to have taken place (as had long before been announced in the press) during this current season in the Malyi Hall of the Conservatoire.[14]

V. E. Meyerhold, with genuinely German hastiness,[15] mobilized all his efforts so as to be first past the post on this occasion: he organized a studio and the journal *Love for Three Oranges*,[16] began to write articles, to give lectures, and so forth – everything so as to appear before the public as quickly as possible, if not in the capacity of initiator, then at least in the role of implementer of the commedia dell'arte's renaissance.

And appear he did. . . . The performance of his pupils and of his camp-followers, at which I chanced to be present,[17] was, to put it simply, in plain Russian, and without any sort of dialectical embellishment – *a performance of the Meyerholdian 'Ancient Theatre'*.

A pre-emptive strike indeed! . . .

Thank you, as they say – I had not expected it! I did expect V. E. Meyerhold to be capable of a great deal in the realm of imitation (take at the very least his 'fascination' with Craigian cubism in the Pinero play *Mid-Channel*[18] or his article 'Farce',[19] which was based on the principle – borrowed from me – of theatricality as the absolute foundation of all scenic art),[20] but for him to have the cheek to borrow wholesale, *without any acknowledgement as to source*, an entire tendency in scenic art created by another – this, I must confess, despite all the vividness of my imagination and my exceptional facility for foresight, I had not expected.

Can it be that V. E. Meyerhold is really so unacquainted with theatrical ethics? With those ethics, which are so strict even as to disallow the borrowing of greasepaint from a fellow-actor without permission? Does he really not understand that a debt outside the jurisdiction of a crown court is regarded in polite society as a sort of 'debt of honour', like a gambling debt, for example?[21]

Of course, I could not take out a patent at the Ministry of Trade for the artistic-reconstructive method, that is to say, for the Ancient Theatre. They do not give out patents for things like that. However, this does not mean that the method originated by me with such an outlay of labour, time, energy, and inspiration is *a matter of no consequence* and, as such, *up for grabs by the first person who comes along!*[22] If V. E. Meyerhold does not know this, then let him hasten to ask some scrupulous legal advisers to give him all the necessary explanations on this score. This is my good counsel. For you know the saying: 'if the jug gets too used to going for water, that's where it will break its neck'.[23]

In the final analysis, I desire nothing but good for V. E. Meyerhold, many of whose productions I consider competent and, most importantly, talented.

True, it is not given to him to be an innovator; for this he is too bogged down in the tricks of his trade, too fussy, too absorbed by his concern to make 'a bigger splash',[24] but mainly because he possesses a character which too easily succumbs to the influence of others.

But all the same he is one of our most talented and cultured directors.

So it is all the more shameful for him (oh, where is his pride?) *to try to be original at someone else's expense! . . .* And when precisely? When it pleased fate, in the great era of patriotic war, to call up for the defence of his native land the valiant Russian warrior K. M. Miklashevskii – one of the really pre-eminent directors and actors of the Ancient Theatre – and thereby to make it morally impossible for this theatre to realize on stage the cycle of commedia dell'arte performances which had been in preparation for the previous three years.[25] Verily, 'all this would be funny, were it not so sad'.

Harlequin the Marriage Broker in 1911. Evreinov, who, despite his 1908 commedia playlet *Veselaya Smert'* (*A Merry Death*), could scarcely claim either anteriority or monopoly in his recourse to commedia, is probably referring to announcements in 1914 in the journal *Love for Three Oranges* (see Note 16 below) that the newly formed Meyerhold Acting Studio planned to devote considerable attention to that particular theatrical form. Once again, Evreinov's paranoia would seem to be outstripping the facts of the case.

13. *Marta La Piedosa* was presented as part of the Ancient Theatre's Spanish Cycle, 28 November 1911.

14. Evreinov is careful to point out that the Ancient Theatre's commedia season had been planned ever since the Spanish season of 1911-12, and had been widely announced in the press. His intention is to cast Meyerhold's rather more recent plans in an inferior, and posterior, light. The 'current season' referred to is 1914–15 (i.e., at the time of Evreinov's authorship of this article).

15. Evreinov is making an unwarranted and slightly unpleasant reference to Meyerhold's Germanic origins. He enlarges on this in his much later (and even more vitriolic) attack in his *Istoriya Russkogo Teatra* (*History of the Russian Theatre*), published posthumously in 1955. There (p. 372), Evreinov vindictively labels Meyerhold 'chistokrov-nym nemtsem' ('pure-blooded German by birth'), and goes out of his way to refer to him by his original name, Karl-Teodore-Kasimir, whose foreign-ness [sic], Evreinov claims, explains a lot about his distant relationship to Russian artists. Evreinov goes on to complain, somewhat pathetically, about his adversary's rampant opportunism, 'his ruthless experimentation at the expense of colleagues, . . . his brazen shifts in artistic positions . . . ', and so on.

16. Meyerhold's own Studio was launched during the 1914-15 season, promising a stage movement curriculum strongly weighted towards classical Spanish drama and Italian commedia dell'arte. This coincided with the appearance of the pseudonymic Doctor Dapertutto's journal *Lyubov k trem apelsinam* (*Love for Three Oranges*, a title taken from Gozzi, the eighteenth-century commedia revivalist), which continued to announce the Studio's activities until the war forced the cessation of both enterprises by early 1917. Meyerhold's organization of all this was so systematic and programmatic that Evreinov' accusations are far from convincing.

17. The Meyerhold Studio's official public debut was on 12 February 1915, and its programme, which included a revival of Blok's commedia playlet *Balaganchik*, was repeated twice during March. The exact date of Evreinov's article, published the same year, is not known, but it would appear that Evreinov was an early attender at the Studio's performances.

18. A reference to Meyerhold's production at the Alexandrinsky Theatre, Petrograd, premiered on 30 January 1914, with designs by Alexander Golovin.

19. 'Balagan' ('Farce'), a long article published in 1912 on theatricality and folk theatre influences.

20. Evreinov provides his own footnote at this point: 'My article "An Apologia for Theatricality" appeared in *Svobodnye Mysly* (*Free Thoughts*), edited by I. M. Vasilevsky in 1908, and Meyerhold's "Farce" in his book *On Theatre* in 1913.' The fact that this book came out at the end of 1912, although its cover is dated 1913, slightly weakens Evreinov's argument.

21. There is a nice irony here, since a few years earlier, in 1912, Evreinov had nominated Meyerhold as one of three members of a specially convened arbitration tribunal to intercede on his behalf in a rather damaging dispute with Baron Driezen, co-founder of the Ancient Theatre. The dispute, like so many of those in which Evreinov became embroiled, had been all about authorial rights and the relative apportionment of credit. In other words Meyerhold – of all people – had, paradoxically, been brought in to help adjudicate in a matter of honour involving Evreinov's entitlement to recognition for originality.

22. In the original article the italicized text appears in Latin: *'res nullius . . . primo occupanti caedit'*. Unless this is a misprint, it would appear that Evreinov has again allowed a grammatical error to creep into his would-be erudition, since the Latin verb 'caedo-caedere', which means 'cut, strike, kill', is inappropriate to the sense. Perhaps he intended 'cado-cadere', meaning 'fall', which would work better.

23. Another proverb used with obscure sarcasm.

24. This is more than a little disingenuous, for the available evidence suggests that Meyerhold's penchant for publicity was nothing compared to Evreinov's!

25. Evreinov is referring again to the unrealized commedia cycle planned for the Ancient Theatre's season at the precise time of writing (1914-15). The main reason for the cancellation had been the call-up of the leading authority K. M. Miklashevskii. Hence, Evreinov seems to be appealing to anti-German sentiment by suggesting that any such season mounted after the war would be compromised by Meyerhold's opportunism. If so, he may well have been mistaking enterprise for plagiarism.

continued from page 324

M. E. Darskii, in which he had received a cutting from the newspaper *Stock Exchange News* announcing the proposed opening by Evreinov of a Studio venture, Meyerhold had written:

What a plagiarist he is! Music, the plastic arts. . . . You know, this is exactly what we're dreaming of for our studio. However, this doesn't scare me! It doesn't take skill to steal an idea, but to implement it is another matter! It takes a certain talent. And it's doubtful whether Evreinov has any![7]

However, Meyerhold's revenge for the attack by Evreinov in 1915 came in 1917 in a review for *Stock Exchange News* of a somewhat sycophantic monograph on Evreinov by the futurist poet Vasilii Kamensky. In this review, Meyerhold retaliates in kind by accusing Evreinov of falsely claiming the invention (in 1909) of the theory of monodrama some time after he, Meyerhold, had employed distinctly monodramatic principles in his 1907 production for Kommissarzhevskaya of Leonid Andreyev's *The Life of a Man*.[8]

Other unflattering references to Evreinov can be found elsewhere in Meyerhold's correspondence. Thus, in September 1917, only a matter of weeks before the October Revolution, Meyerhold wrote to Alexander Tairov of Moscow's Kamernyi Theatre about an agreement – notwithstanding personal feelings – between Meyerhold, Tairov, and Evreinov to establish a new experimental theatre in Moscow where all three luminaries would work with equal creative autonomy. Apparently, Meyerhold was to have sent Tairov the text of a press interview given jointly by himself and Evreinov in Petrograd announcing the venture. However, he wrote:

I'm not sending the interview because N. N. Evreinov is in no way able to bestir himself in this matter. We see each other every Sunday. I'm at a loss to comprehend why he is prevaricating. I strongly advise you to write to him, reminding him of his promise. Write that the matter is urgent and very important for the Kamernyi Theatre.[9]

This unlikely joint venture never got off the ground.

Later still, in his booklet *The Reconstruction of the Theatre* (1929-30), Meyerhold again made negative reference to his old adversary (by now in Parisian exile) and was able to imply a stinging political criticism. Writing about the gap between what the theatre and the street had to offer, Meyerhold then continues:

It reminds me of a director who once caused such a stir here with his paradoxical books and articles on the theatre: Evreinov. I recall his eccentricity, his desire to dramatize life. I should have thought that he would find it easy enough to realize his dream in a town like Paris where the dramatization of life seems such a practical possibility. He need only go to the Place d'Italie, join the workers in their self-composed songs, and set about directing them. It's a pity that he's not prepared to move out of the émigré quarter of Passy to a working-class district.[10]

Evreinov's subsequent recollections of Meyerhold turned out to be even less favourable. In his quirky and subjective *A History of the Russian Theatre* (1953), Evreinov displays possibly even more rancour towards his nemesis than in the article reproduced here.[11] In fact, some sections of this are so venomous that they do their author no credit, especially taking into account Meyerhold's terminal struggle with the Stalinist machine.

Though Evreinov acknowledges Meyerhold's centrality to any history of Russian theatre (despite the attempts of Stalinist criticism to pretend otherwise), he repeats his old arguments about plagiarism, complains at some length about Meyerhold's Germanic origins, and implies that his enthusiasm for Bolshevism was inordinately opportunistic.

Evreinov even seems to seek a perverse satisfaction in the official charges of 'Meyerholditis' which befell his adversary in the difficult days of 1936. In a proud reference back to 'Originality at Someone Else's Expense', he quotes selectively, as if in final proof of his influence on Meyerhold, from the conclusion of Eduard Stark, the historian of *Ancient Theatre*:

From the Spanish Golden Age season of Evreinov's Ancient Theatre, 1911-12. Top: design sketch by A. K. Shervashidze for *Martha the Pious*. Bottom: photo of the court scene in Lope de Vega's *Fuente Ovejuna*.

Meyerhold's Petrograd Studio, with all its achievements in the field of the actor's plasticity, the passion for Gozzi and Hoffman, the whole business of *Love for Three Oranges* and the other analogous phenomena, what were these things if not the direct consequence of everything achieved by the *Ancient Theatre*?[12]

Evreinov, in what was one of his very last evaluations of Meyerhold, did considerably tone down his antipathy, and was even prepared to discuss his rival's achievements in a more objective light. In a very long three-part article, 'There Were Four of Us', which appeared in the French émigré journal *Vozrozhdeniye* in 1952, Evreinov paid Meyerhold the tribute of being the first among equals, claiming that the four leading lights of the Russian avant-garde theatre had been Meyerhold, Evreinov, Fyodor Kommissarzhevsky, and Alexander Tairov, *in that order*.[13]

Nor was this the only example of Evreinov's inconsistency, despite everything, in his relations with Meyerhold. In 1912, unlikely as it may seem, he had nominated Meyerhold as his arbitrator in a complex legal dispute about author's rights.[14] In the period 1915 to 1919 both men had been involved with Boris Pronin and others in the establishment of the Petrograd bohemian artistic cabaret *The Comedian's Halt*, which was the successor to the better known *Stray Dog*. Finally, in 1921, when Meyerhold's stock in the Soviet theatre establishment was at its height, he held out a collegiate olive branch to Evreinov when he sent him an urgent telegram in the following words:

Proposition return Moscow, guaranteed a flat and removal of furniture and library. You will take RSFSR theatre No. 2, I'll take RSFSR No. 1. Reply at once in affirmative. Meyerhold.[15]

Evreinov's wife was keen to accept, but Evreinov refused. Perhaps he had too many old scores with Meyerhold. What their collaboration might have yielded no one will ever know.

According to Evreinov's widow, the two men had one last encounter, years later – almost certainly in September 1930 – in Paris, where Meyerhold and his wife had gone for a visit. By chance the Evreinovs sighted the Meyerholds in a cinema queue. Spencer Golub describes this poignant moment as follows:

Coincidentally, Evreinov and Meyerhold turned in each other's direction at the same instant, and their eyes met. Each made a movement in the other's direction as if to exchange salutations, but in the next moment, stopped short, turned back to their respective lines and passed into the theatre without saying a word to one another. They avoided each other on the way out as well. It was their last chance at a reconciliation.[16]

Acknowledgements

This article was originally published as 'Original'nost' za chuzhoi schet', in *Zhurnal Zhurnalov* (*Journal of Journals*), No. 1, Petrograd (1915), p. 15-16. This translation © 1989 by Tony Pearson, with thanks to Martin Dewhirst of the University of Glasgow for invaluable advice on translation and to Lesley Milne of the University of Nottingham for obtaining the scarce original from the Lenin Library, Moscow.

Notes and References

1. See Spencer Golub, *Evreinov: the Theatre of Paradox and Transformation* (Ann Arbor, Michigan, 1984), p. 137 and p. 186-90.

2. V. E. Meyerhold, 'Literaturnye predvestiya o novom teatre' ('The New Theatre Foreshadowed in Literature'), first published in *Teatr: kniga o novom teatre* (*Theatre: a Book about the New Theatre*, Petersburg, 1908), trans. Edward Braun, in *Meyerhold on Theatre* (London, 1969), p. 34.

3. V. E. Meyerhold, *O Teatre* (*On the Theatre*, Petersburg, 1913), p. 28-9.

4. Vyacheslav Ivanov, 'Nenuzhnaya pravda' ('The Unnecessary Truth'), *Mir Iskusstva* (*The World of Art*), No. 4 (1902), cited in V. E. Meyerhold, 'The Stylized Theatre', first published in *Teatr: kniga o novom teatre*, 1908, and translated in Braun, op. cit., p. 58.

5. Golub, op. cit., p. 163.

6. C. Moody, p. xxv of Introduction to Bradda edition of N. N. Evreinov, *Istoriya Russkogo Teatra* (*A History of the Russian Theatre*, n.d.), assembled in its Russian language version in 1953 from an earlier French work (*L'Histoire du théâtre russe*, 1947) and published posthumously in 1955.

7. V. E. Meyerhold, letter to M. E. Darskii, 30 July 1908, in *Perepiska (1896-1939)* (*Correspondence*, Moscow, 1976), p. 115, 377-8.

8. V. E. Meyerhold, 'Retsenziya' ('Review'), *Birzhevye Vedomosti* (*Stock Exchange News*), 10 Feb. 1917, cited in Golub, op. cit., p. 251.

9. V. E. Meyerhold, letter to Tairov, 13 Sept. 1917, in *Perepiska*, op. cit., p. 189, 396.

10. V. E. Meyerhold, 'Rekonstruktsiya teatra' ('The Reconstruction of the Theatre'), 1929-30, in V. E. Meyerhold, *Stati, Pis'ma, Rechi, Besedy II, 1917-1939* (*Articles, Letters, Speeches, Conversations*, Moscow 1968), translated in Braun, op. cit., p. 264.

11. N. N. Evreinov, *Istoriya Russkogo Teatra*, op. cit., p. 363-94.

12. Eduard Stark, *Starinnyi Teatr* (*The Ancient Theatre*, Petersburg, 1922), p. 70-1, cited in N. N. Evreinov, *Istoriya Russkogo Teatra*, op. cit., p. 393.

13. N. N. Evreinov, 'Nas bylo chetvero: o teatre pod sovetskoi feruloi' ('There were Four of Us: about the Theatre under Soviet Rule'), *Vozrozhdeniye* (*Resurrection*), Paris, XXI (1952), p. 82-94; XXII, p. 116-32; XXIII, p. 89-101.

14. See Golub, op. cit., p. 137, and C. Moody, 'Nikolai Nikolaevich Evreinov, 1879-1953', *Russian Literature Triquarterly*, No. 13 (Fall 1975), p. 678-80.

15. V. E. Meyerhold, telegram to N. N. Evreinov, Autumn 1921. See Anna Kashina-Evreinova, *Evreinov v mirovom teatre xx veka* (*Evreinov in the World Theatre of the Twentieth Century*, Paris, 1964), p. 16.

16. Golub, op. cit., p. 210.

Peter Elsass

The Healing Space in Psychotherapy and Theatre

This article is a comparative examination of the relationship of audience and actors on the one hand, and of a client and his psychotherapist on the other. Peter Elsass argues that in order to describe both relationships as of a healing nature, one also has to identify a 'healing space' beyond the consulting room, instead of focusing on the healing relationship itself. Employing an analogy with shamanism, he describes this 'healing space' as a 'pinta', or vision from an extra-contextual frame. The history of psychoanalysis shows this need for a 'pinta' as a driving, rebellious force, and he suggests that without a 'pinta' of its own, the theatre also dies. Peter Elsass is a Professor of Health Psychology in the Medical Faculty of Aarhus University, Denmark, and chief psychologist at the Psychiatric Hospital, Aarhus. In addition to writing a large number of articles within the medical and psychological fields, he has also worked in the field of cultural anthropology, and in *Strategies for Survival: the Psychology of Cultural Resilience in Ethnic Minorities* (New York University Press, 1992), he describes his many periods of residence with Indian tribes in Colombia. Peter Elsass has been an associate of Odin Theatre, and has taught at the International School of Theatre Anthropology, directed by Eugenio Barba.

NUMEROUS ATTEMPTS have been made to combine the study of theatre with that of psychotherapy. Most have been unsuccessful. Some have been filled with a romantic love for the theatre on the part of the psychotherapist, a feeling which has rarely been reciprocated. There are many reasons for this unproductive attraction – one of them being the apparent similarity between the work of actors and psychotherapists, both of whom share the aim of creating new insights or making implicit knowledge explicit for the audience or patients.

Both struggle with the problem of creating change through a fixed method. The theatre brings about change by means of repetition: for how can the actors maintain the necessary intensity when they have to stage the same performance night after night? Similarly, the psychotherapist has to work with the repetitive repertoire of the patient's problems: for how can the therapist remain engaged with a method which calls upon the patient to live and relive the same problem session after session?

The shared problem of finding a creative focal point in their work may have escalated the attraction between theatre people and therapists, both longing for creative stimulation in their repetitive work. The therapists certainly long for stimulating literature instead of boring patients, and perhaps the actors need to consider their audience as patients when their critical response is too wounding.

There may be many other reasons for the attraction between theatre and therapy. Both theatre and therapy thus work with 'the other' via the instrument of themselves. Since skilled therapists must themselves have been through therapy, they literally use themselves in their concern for 'the other'. The principle of professional identity cannot exist without the presence of the other, and sometimes the community of therapists turn into 'clubs', sharing theories of 'otherness'. A similar narcissistic attitude can be found in theatre life, where the hidden secrets are created and made visible through 'the work of the actor with himself,' as Stanislavsky has put it.

It is easy to be ironic about these 'temples of otherness', where actors and therapists create knowledge of the other by working with themselves. In the century of narcissism, a common space between theatre and therapy has become loaded with seductive feelings which must be entered with caution.

One way to defend oneself as a researcher in this loaded area has been to take as a basis existing studies of 'ritual' and 'ceremonies'. Some such analytical steps have been stimulating, while others have been merely reductionist, denying that there are fundamental differences between theatre and therapy. There is an enormous literature of rituals, performances, and ceremonies, in which the current trend is in danger of becoming too methodological and self-absorbed. To quote Freud: 'Those who limit their studies to methodological investigations remind me of people who are always polishing their glasses instead of putting them on and seeing with them' (Reik, 1940, p. 138).

Bearing this in mind, I want to analyze the healing relationship in both theatre and therapy. Moving directly into the subject without many references to the anthropology of rituals, ceremonies, and performances, I will attempt to define the core of the creative process through the essential relationships between client and therapist and between audience and actor.

The Context of the Debate

My intention is to discuss some aspects of that particular contextualization created between the two parties which both in therapy and theatre produces 'life and insight'. Through this discussion, I shall seek to investigate and question the degree of common understanding between the two parties necessary to produce effective healing – or a good performance.

I am not going to elaborate what I mean by 'healing' and 'good performance' until later. Provisionally, 'healing' and 'good performance' imply that something has been created which was not there before. This 'something' may be called 'insight' in psychotherapy or 'the holy invisible' in theatre.

One of the central questions within the theatre is how to create a kind of life which does not exist in the 'real life' situation.

Within the impossible profession of psychotherapy, there are parallel descriptions of how a state of insight provides more freedom and life. Some therapeutic activities are more active and suggestive in creating this insight: others, such as the psychoanalytical, are more passive, producing a state of Hegelian insight.

A general question concerning these different therapeutic activities is the degree to which there should be a sort of congruency or complementarity in the relationship between client and therapist. In communication theory, 'congruency' means a common understanding created by sharing the same experience, while 'complementarity,' refers to a common understanding created by the difference between the communicating parties. The question is, then, to what degree is healing produced on the basis of difference or sameness?

The same question is sometimes asked in theatre life. Some theatres seem to aim for a maximum degree of congruency – for example, the traditional theatre with a fixed repertoire which Peter Brook has called 'the deadly theatre', where the actors provide the audience with the experience they expect (Brook, 1968). Similarly, there are therapists who take on the role of the sympathetic listener, always following the patient in his 'slipstream,' achieving a nice encounter, possibly with some insight as a result, but with no transformation outside the therapeutic room.

Other theatres place themselves in a position of incomprehensibility, where they perform independently of the audience, thereby gradually destroying themselves. Similarly, some therapists adopt an occult, almost shamanistic position, where the client does not understand a single word of the wild therapeutic interventions and is seduced into an experience of a sort of healing.

If a performance has to be created, or a healing has to occur, the ritual in both cases requires the making explicit of an implicit knowledge: this is what creates the mutual understanding in both cases. The context of the ritual will be different depending on the choice of either the congruent or the complementary relationship. My hypothesis is that both relationships may be productive in bringing about either a performance or a healing if the actor or the therapist has an outer vision which he experiences as a kind of truth and meaning. Without this, no implicit knowledge will be revealed. We know this all too well from experience.

Without a vision, neither the performance nor the therapy will have an empowering effect on their 'objects'. To establish some firm ground under this hypothesis, I shall introduce a concept from medical research.

Compliance and Non-Compliance

The medical concept of *compliance* refers to differing degrees or stages of power-sharing in the practitioner-patient relationship. It derives from the Latin *compliere*, which means both to follow and to complement, and refers to the clinical situation where the patient follows the doctor's advice. Other terms that have been used are 'adherence', 'obedience', 'co-operation', 'concordance', 'collaboration' or 'therapeutic alliance', each representing a different point along the authoritarian-democratic scale. These terms are used interchangeably, depending upon the ideology of the patient-doctor relationship. Generally, compliance reflects an overtly authoritative approach to patient care, implying an obligation on the part of the patient to follow the practitioner's orders blindly (DiMateo and DiNicola, 1982, p. 9).

Research has shown that generally about 40 per cent of patients do not follow the medical advice given. It has been a shock for the medical profession to realize that although medical research is so rational and empirically based, an alarming proportion of patients do not comply with the doctor's advice, and thousands of publications on the theme have been produced since the beginning of the 1960s (see, for example, the reviews by Thompson, 1984, and Lassen, 1989). For advice on life quality and preventive medicine, the rate of non-compliance has been as high as 90 per cent.

In the beginning, most of the literature about non-compliance discussed this as a fault on the part of the patient. That view still represents the authoritarian position, but many researchers have now changed their focus, seeking to look at the total situation in all its social, cultural, ethical, and psychological aspects: this has produced a host of theories about non-compliance.

From a psychological point of view, it has been argued that non-compliance may express the patient's rejection of authority in an attempt to regain control of a situation which has in reality been difficult to control because of the character of the disease. It is a way of becoming independent of the therapist who is able to give new and disturbing information about the disease – a psychological defence mechanism against a frightening collaboration.

In a wider perspective, non-compliance may be taken as a sort of power game on the medical battlefield about who has the right to advise another person and who has to comply with whom. Thus, from the patient's point of view, the medical staff does not comply with his needs when, for example, there are long waiting lists for treatment, or too small waiting rooms for too long waits.

There are many other examples of doctors not following their patients' 'advice'. Some studies have shown that around 20 per cent of hospitalized patients are in hospital because of a side effect of medical treatment; and here non-compliance can be seen as a correct response to an inappropriate treatment (Ausburn, 1981).

Non-compliance thus has its reasons, which patient and doctor must investigate together. One of the most convincing studies indicates that the more information a doctor has about his patient's non-compliance, the better are the possibilities of enhancing collaboration in the treatment. Mutual understanding of the reasons for non-compliance gives a better outcome.

These studies of compliance provide stimulating possibilities for further reflection on the ideology inherent in the patient-doctor relationship. What does it mean to say that doctor and patient are satisfied with a consultation and a treatment? Who is responsible for the outcome, and how does one measure a satisfying outcome? Some patients do not want a treatment and are satisfied without it, but the doctor labels them as non-compliers.

Congruency

The concept of 'compliance' thus reflects a performance of power within the relationship between patients and therapists. Compliance is the end-result of the consultation process. It can be obtained in different ways, by congruency or complementarity. But the dominant trend in the studies of compliance has given priority to congruency, the democratic ideology being to equalize the power relationship or to redefine it, thus rationalizing the doctor's authoritative status. He is seen as the knowing person, who has an instrumental knowledge to offer the patient, while the patient has a status of being in an autonomous position which has to be respected.

There are some interesting examples of how non-compliance can be very provocative for society, even if the non-compliant behaviour is in accord with the idea of autonomy and self-determination. Bouvia's case from California is perhaps well known. A multi-handicapped patient decided not to accept any form of treatment, and even refused food. Many self-help groups expressed outrage over how a handicapped patient could choose to be handicapped in the wrong way. A 'good' handicapped person should argue: 'I have a handicap, but I am glad that I'm alive' (Brody, 1987, p. 131).

Another example is from the diary of Peter Noll, who, suffering from cancer, decided not to receive any treatment, even though there was a good chance that the disease might have been cured. One of his friends said: 'You provoke our indignation. You show us that death is present among us, and you show it to us in a living condition, with the result that we have to reflect about something we have always denied' (Noll, 1984, p. 41).

The dominant ideology within medical treatment is to view it as a kind of welfare work, where the patient takes responsibility for his situation – but on the premise that it must not disturb others. In the earlier 'machine-model', the patient was seen as a passive recipient of caring, and had to surrender his body to the treatment without any responsibility for the result. By contrast the welfare model is based on the premise of active patients, prepared for a mutual collaboration in their treatment.

Two recent Danish doctoral theses have demonstrated how important it is for the result of the treatment that the power relationship between staff and patients be equalized. Lunde has stated that the general practitioner has to take as his point of reference the patient's own experience of the disease, if compliance is to be achieved (Lunde, 1990), while Salling has demonstrated that the nursing staff has to involve the patient in preparing and organizing his hospital stay (Salling, 1990).

The 'democratic consultation' is part of an ideology of congruency between the patients' and the doctors' models. It seems to be too simple, however, to account for the healing that takes place in the space between them. In Greenland, for instance, I have found hospital patients who were not at all interested in taking any active responsibility for their situation, since they come from a cultural tradition where the family as a whole normally takes that responsibility rather than a single member. Again, if a family has a lot of problems with alcohol and violence, one of its members sometimes gets sick and pleads for hospitalization as a kind of rehabilitation, to regain mental peace and order. When young and idealistic Danish doctors demanded that the individual patients should take the situation into their own hands and be responsible, the result was non-compliance.

The ideology of equalizing the patient-doctor relationship can be an excuse for the professional not taking responsibility himself, instead delegating the problems to the family, for example – the very social context which the patient wants to get rid of for a period of time. The point is that a congruent relationship based on shared understanding does not necessarily give better opportunities for healing than a relationship of complementarity, where the differences between the parties provoke new insight.

Complementarity

We have some ideological difficulties in accepting the relationship of complementarity in this sense, because it has associations to power and suppression. But we often do need differences for creating a good healing performance. In theatre, too, the equalizing of power between the audience and the actors does not necessarily give a better performance.

Keith Johnstone's remarks about 'status' in his *Impro* (1986) are impressive in this respect. I myself have seen him working with actors, and been forced to realize how adding a status difference between two actors gave life and presence to their acting. And I have seen actors working in a democratic relationship with their audience, their director, and each other, only for a different sort of life and presence to emerge when they were put into a position of resistance – as it might be, when they were quarrelling, when their message to the audience did not come through, or when the social institution did not support them. The content of this resistance is manifold, but one of its aspects is that the tension creates a sort of difference among the parts either in the physical world or in the mental images produced. That difference can give rise to an energy which in turn produces a more interesting theatre.

One can find similar examples in the medical world. There are some consultations in which patients and doctors do not understand each other, where there is very little mutuality and almost no collaboration between the parties, but where healing none the less takes place. Thus, in my work in Greenland I have seen many examples of patients recovering very quickly from surgery and other acute states of illness, even if they did not understand a single word of the Danish nurses and doctors.

Directly questioned, these patients said that they were not interested in getting information about their disease and its treatment: several said that it was the doctor who had this knowledge, and that he, therefore, must be responsible for the treatment, in which they had full confidence. An interesting phenomenon was that most of the 50 Danish nurses and doctors said that the Greenlandic patients recovered more rapidly than Danish patients, had fewer complaints about side effects, and were sooner back to work.

Of course, this has to be analyzed in a broader context than just that of communication between doctor and patient. The social context, the culture, and the cosmology of disease, all have to be considered. The point is, however, that in some contexts a complementary relationship between patient and healer can give positive results, even if the patient and the healer do not understand each other. Similarly, a theatre can give a good performance even if the audience does not understand a single word.

The Greenlandic example reminds me of an example given by Lévi-Strauss of the use and the efficacy of a Cuna Indian shaman's healing of a woman in obstructed labour. Even though the woman did not understand a single word of the song, it worked very well (Lévi-Strauss, 1967, p. 161).

Anthropologists, of course, know that a broader contextualization is necessary to understand the effectiveness of the shamanistic healing. Similarly, in the Greenlandic example a broadening of the context of communication between doctors and patients allows us to understand why the patients were cured more speedily than the Danish patients. When you take all aspects of the consultation into account, you will understand the meaning it has, but an all-embracing contextualizing may be a form of neutralizing its aspects.

From a psychotherapeutic viewpoint, the healing power between a Danish doctor and a Greenlandic patient could be explained by the doctor's use of 'supportive techniques'. When the doctor exhibits an authority figure to the patient, there will be possibilities for the patient to project and transfer his fear of disease to the doctor, so that for a short period of time he has an unrealistic experience of being helped. This explanation of supportive techniques might be expanded by introducing some aspects of shamanistic healing – which is fundamentally a supportive technique, but is also more than that.

Shamanistic Healing

As noted by Lévi-Strauss, the shaman may cure people by providing them with a mythic language in which to express pain and confusion. He thus notes that 'the cure would consist . . . in making explicit a situation originally existing on the emotional level, and in rendering acceptable to the mind pains which the body refuses to tolerate' (Lévi-Strauss, 1979, p. 323). Like the psychoanalyst, the shaman acts as protagonist in the drama and as a sympathetic listener. In inducing the patient to live out the myth, he uses metaphor to tap deep problems and lighten the mental anguish.

Myth itself works toward mediating oppositions and makes all things possible. The shaman acts as a cosmic trickster, bringing the past into the present, shuffling cause and effect, and mediating life and death. In brief: the shaman brings back knowledge to his people.

It is difficult to compare shamanism with psychotherapy – even more difficult than to compare theatre with therapy. But instead of a comparison, one can attempt an analogy in order to find a clue to the working mechanisms in therapy. The difference between plain psychotherapy, even when it is supportive or explorative, and shamanism is that the latter adds a new experience to the patient in the form of a vision which the patient did not have before. Whether in therapy or shamanism, healing is a consequence of giving the patient this vision, even if psychotherapy does it in a more repressed and hidden way than shamanism.

This new experience which the healing process brings into being cannot be understood by broadening the context, because it is something coming from outside – from a field outside the previous context of the patient. It derives from an 'extra-contextual space', so to speak. Let me substantiate that by referring to the work of Taussig. He says that the song of the shaman as a text is ripped out of any world, but has its own internal referentiality (Taussig, 1987, p. 390). The shaman tames savagery – not to eliminate it, but to acquire it. The power of shamanism lies not with the shaman, but with the differences created by the coming together of shaman and patient – differences constituting an imagery essential to the articulation of what one can call implicit social knowledge.

An essential aspect of the shamanistic process is the shaman's experience of a vision – a 'pinta' – to which he gives the patient access. Normally, the shaman uses some sort of medicine which has a visionary capacity to stimulate the healing to give the sick person insight into the cause of his misfortune and power to overcome it. However, this healing power does not necessarily come from seeing the actual causes of misfortune, but from having a particular image – a 'pinta', or a painting, as it is commonly referred to. To become a healer is to buy and to acquire such a pinta; it may happen through the use of a medicine-induced vision (Taussig, 1990, p. 213).

As in the shamanistic process, the healing relationship in psychotherapy cannot always be understood by simple contextualization. Here, too, we must find a 'pinta', or vision, a truth deriving from outside the space between the doctor and the patient. To understand the healing relationship one must refer to a context other than the implicit social knowledge between doctor and patient.

The patient-doctor relationship often creates a new truth in the patient: it is not simply a digging out of what was already hidden in the unconscious. In other words, the healing relationship creates a new reality: it not only deduces, it also induces. Similarly theatre does not simply transform ordinary life to a new kind of experience: a good performance sometimes creates an entirely new reality. That is what gives meaning to working in the theatre: in the same way, the creation of an entirely new reality in the patient and doctor is what produces the healing.

From a psychoanalytical point of view, the idea of giving the patient a vision involves a completely non-analytical attitude. Shamanism inverts the psychoanalytic technique to achieve abreaction, since in shamanism it is not the patient's but the shaman's speech that fills the therapeutic space.

The idea of the psychotherapist is not to intrude his own attitude into the patient. Rather, Freud recommended that the psychoanalyst should be like a mirror to his patient (1912). This has been misunderstood to mean that the psychoanalyst should be cold and unresponsive to his patient: but the reference to the mirror rather implies that the analyst's behaviour and attitude in the patient's neurotic conflicts should be 'opaque', so that it reflects back to the patient nothing but what the patient himself manifests, into the analysis of which the analyst's personal values and preferences should not intrude. Only by being mute and relatively anonymous to the patient can the transference reactions come into focus and be distinguished from more realistic reactions.

There is no doubt that the less the patient really knows about the psychoanalyst, the more easily he can fill in the blank spaces with his own fantasies. Furthermore, the easier it becomes for the analyst to convince the patient that his reactions are displacements and projections (Greenson, 1967, p. 274). The problem with this method concerns how a psychotherapist can use this 'pinta' without being supportive and losing the analytical possibilities of neutrality.

There are many examples of how psychotherapy comes to an end when a therapist's personal attitude intrudes. Greenson gives the following example of a patient suffering from stomach ulcers and depression (1967, p. 273).

He had been a lifelong Republican (which I had known), and he had tried in recent months to adopt a more liberal point of view, because he knew I was so inclined. I asked him how he knew I was a liberal and anti-Republican. He then told me that whenever he said anything favourable about a Republican politician, I always asked for associations. On the other hand, whenever he said anything hostile about a Republican, I remained silent, as though in agreement. Whenever he had a kind word for Roosevelt, I said nothing. Whenever he attacked Roosevelt, I would ask who did Roosevelt remind him of, as though I was out to prove that hating Roosevelt was infantile.

I was taken aback because I had been completely unaware of this pattern. Yet, the moment the patient pointed it out, I had to agree that I had done precisely that, albeit unknowingly. We then went to work on why he felt the need to try to swallow my political views. This turned out to be his way of ingratiating himself with me. This proved to be indigestible and also lowered his self-esteem, leading to the ulcer symptoms and the depressiveness. (Greenson, 1967, p. 273)

I am sure the theatre people can give similar examples of how a theatre which makes its personal political views explicit may also provoke ulcer symptoms and depression in its audiences.

The Pinta

The problem with both theatre and psychotherapy is how to relate to a kind of 'pinta'. As a vision, the 'pinta' is largely unspeakable: it may never become explicit to anybody during the process, but both parties in either the theatrical or therapeutic process must know of its existence. It is very difficult to reveal the 'pinta'. In the shamanistic process it is the healer who gives the vision, and that is what the shaman most truly sees. But it seems that in truly 'seeing', he cannot or will not speak very much of what he sees: that is why the shaman needs the patient, just as the patient, for perhaps more obvious reasons, needs the shaman. The patient is to be the voice of the shaman.

The problem in qualifying the phenomenon of a hidden meaning called a 'pinta' is that it cannot be approached by expanding the context of the theatrical and therapeutic situation. To concretize this point, let me refer to a study I am conducting with a group of general practitioners who are utilizing psychotherapy with their patients, and in which I interview both patients and doctors after the therapy has come to an end, asking them to tell me about the process.

Many of the results are very interesting. One of them is that the doctors are doing very good work, even though they have no regular psychotherapeutic educational background. Of course, to qualify therapeutic work as 'very good' is difficult, because therapy is difficult to evaluate: but the end result might, say, be an insight and veracity which does not always provoke change in the symptoms of the patients – one of whom told me, for example, that he did not feel he was getting any help from the therapy in the first place. It was a waste of time: every time he asked the doctor for concrete help – that is, for a prescription of tranquillizers – the doctor refused, nor did he even give a single bit of advice. He was so silent, said the patient, that there was no possibility of being dependent on him. He had to listen to himself instead and take the responsibility for his own life. After only one year he could appreciate this result of the therapy.

Although the result of the therapy is difficult to evaluate, it was obvious to all of the participants that it was meaningful for them and had helped them. The general practitioners said that it gave more meaning to their own work, and most of the patients stated that even if it was hard work, it had given them insight into their lives, and more freedom to make some important choices.

But the most striking result was that when analyzing the interview transcripts there was very little congruency between the doctor's and the patient's formulations about the same therapeutic process. In some cases, it was almost impossible from looking at the transcript to believe that they had been talking about the same therapy. Again, this confirmed that healing can take place without a compliance based on a shared understanding of the content of the process.

I have found the same results in a study I am doing with torture victims and psychotherapists. Here, the differences between the statements are even greater, because of the distances in culture between the parties, yet an effective healing of the torture trauma none the less took place.

Perhaps the shared understanding belongs to an outer context, where both parties

experience the therapy as meaningful. Other studies of therapy have shown similar results. When young enthusiastic therapists are sometimes seen to do surprisingly effective work in comparison with older, more experienced therapists, it is thus their greater enthusiasm and stress on meaningfulness that has made made them compare so favourably (Hougaard, 1989).

This 'meaningfulness', 'enthusiasm', or whatever we call it, has been referred to as a 'non-specific factor' because it is not possible to specify precisely the mechanism which had the impact on the therapeutic process (Hougaard, 1989). Even when one can give good reasons for going into psychotherapy, it is difficult to understand concretely how this 'non-specific factor' affects the results – and neither the doctors nor the patients in my investigation ever referred to it when asked about effective mechanisms.

In the context of my previous statements about the 'pinta', it can, then, be argued that some part of the social context has an impact that is never mentioned. A 'pinta' for the psychotherapist is a form of coherence and meaning in his own life which makes it necessary for him to do his work, although this cannot be spelled out.

Gained Truth and Lost Meaning

This argument about the significance of the 'pinta' in psychotherapy and theatre reflects some tendencies within both fields. In recent decades, both theatre and psychotherapy in Europe have been criticized not only for having turned 'legitimate and respectable', but also, in part, for becoming 'sluggish and smug'. In their histories they have not lost their truths but have proceeded by integrating past insights: in so doing, however, they have lost their original ability to convince and to attract attention. They have been deprived of their referent, and even when they have gained truth they have lost meaning. One could thus say that there are many examples of both theatre and therapy having lost their 'pinta'.

Within the area of psychoanalysis, it has been argued that before the analysts' emigration to the USA and England, many of them were politically in opposition, and psychoanalysis itself was even rebellious. But as fascism drove the psychoanalysts out of Europe, psychoanalysis has been criticized for becoming insular, medical, and clinical, and for surrendering the cultural terrain that Freud had staked out (Jacoby, 1986, p. 9). In the 1920s and 1930s psychoanalysts were rebellious intellectuals with broad cultural and political commitments: but in the 1940s and 1950s they matured, and thus became part of the profession's own repression.

Literary critics praised Freud for a 'limpid and forthright style': he wrote simply and elegantly for a wide cultural audience. But today psychoanalytical writing has turned into 'a technical and medical prose', where contemporary analysts complacently write for one another (Jacoby, 1986, p. 101). And psychoanalysis itself has become a fashionable treatment for fashionable ailments (Malcolm, 1982).

The early psychoanalysts who identified themselves as socialists and Marxists – including Paul Federn, Helene Deutsch, Siegfred Bernfeld, Herman Nunberg, Annie and Wilhelm Reich, Edith Jacobsen, Bruno Bettelheim, Ernst Simmel, and Fenichel – may even have constituted a majority of the profession. But the insecurity of those who were political refugees in the United States made them want to avoid attention. Not only did American psychoanalysts become cautious, but the repression was so strong that they lost their political and cultural commitments in the process of their Americanization.

This spoiled their 'pinta'. To remain a vital force, knowledge requires living contact between teachers and students. Knowledge is bathed in emotions, desires, and commitments. Without these nurturing fluids, it withers into empty words. The texts were saved, but they lost their urgency.

Such broad generalizations about the state of psychoanalysis, as of any discipline, are of course suspect. Next to every pronouncement of decline and crisis may be found congratulations and self congratula-

tions concerning recent advances. And it should be mentioned that psychoanalysis is again a living and rebellious force within psychology: thus, the Frankfurt School is an example of how psychoanalysis kept alive while remaining loyal to social theory. There are many such examples of revitalization, in the work of Adornos *et al.*, Marcuse, and Norman O. Brown, and in more recent years Bruckner and Ziehe. I could also mention the powerful neo-Freudian movements of the 1960s.

Yet if we focus on the 1940s and 1950s there are many signs of decline. After the 1930s, the era of literary and bohemian adventuring into the unconscious was coming to an end. In 1955, the president of the American Psychoanalytic Association thus declared of the new graduates: 'They are not so introspective, are inclined to read only the literature that is assigned . . . and wish to get through with the training requirements as rapidly as possible' (Knight, 1963, in Jacoby, 1986, p. 141).

The forces that guided this Americanization of the psychoanalytical movement can roughly be identified as: professionalization and medicalization; the insecurity of refugee analysts; the gap between American and European culture, and – as cause and effect – the emergence of the neo-Freudians.

In the 1940s and 1950s, the psychoanalytic landscape appeared to break down into different terrains, where the political and rebellious Freudians languished in the shadows of the conservatives. Those few people, such as Adorno, Fenichel, and Lindner, who survived with a public identity to become reference points in contemporary culture, preserved their rebellious perspectives by toning down their radicalism: 'They said alienation when they meant capitalism, reason when they meant revolution, and Eros when they meant proletariat' (Jacoby, 1986, p. 151). In this way, they assured their underground survival during the McCarthy period.

Transmission of culture is a fragile affair. Basic scientific knowledge can eventually be recovered from texts, but other elements depend more heavily on emotional colouring and human contact. If a certain degree of urgency is not communicated by teachers or does not resonate in students, these cultural impulses dissipate. That happened for some part of American psychoanalysis – which flourished, but now as a decultured trade, in which only a few isolated rebels survived.

Some claim that this repression is still a basic characteristic of American psychoanalysis (Jacoby, 1986; Mason, 1990). In the loss of some of its fundamental vigorous force, in the terms of my argument it has lost its 'pinta'. And – the reason for my telling the story – the same could be argued about some parts of the theatre. Eugenio Barba has said that it is as if theatre people 'are moving in darkness, that they do not feel what sort of meaning it has' (Barba 1986).

The Healing Space

Theatre is not like therapy, but one can use performance in either field as an analogy for the other. Both have a premise which assumes a relationship to another part: actor to audience, therapist to patient. But the fundamental issue is not the power relationship between those two parties, whether based in congruency or complementarity. The main issue is the contextual frame, where a vision outside the implicit social knowledge – a 'pinta' – is brought into being.

This 'pinta,' or whatever we choose to call it, does not belong to the relationship between patient and therapist, and cannot be understood by (for example) theories of transference and counter-transference. A healing can be created both in a relationship of congruency and of complementarity. For the understanding of the healing relationship one has to add a space beyond the therapeutic room, and even outside so-called implicit social knowledge.

One has to identify the healing space instead of focusing on the healing relationship. By analogy with shamanism, I have called this healing space a 'pinta' – a vision

coming from another reality, from an extra-contextual frame. The history of psychoanalysis shows this need for a 'pinta' as a driving, rebellious force, and the situation of theatre demonstrates that without a 'pinta' the theatre also will be dead.

References

Ausburn, L., 'Patient Compliance with Medication Regimens', in Sheppard, J., ed., *Behavioral Medicine* (Cumberland College of Health Sciences, 1981).

Barba, E., *Beyond the Floating Islands* (New York: PAJ Publications, 1986).

Barba, E., 'Teatret som et skrig pa brod', *Information*, No. 26 (Sept. 1988).

Brody, H., *Stories of Sickness* (Yale University Press, 1987).

Brook, P., *The Empty Space* (London, 1968).

DiMatteo, M. R., and DiNicola, D. D., *Achieving Patient Compliance: the Psychology of the Medical Practitioner's Role* (New York: Pergamon Press, 1982).

Freud, S., *Recommendations to Physicians Practising Psychoanalysis*, Standard Edition, XII (1927), p. 109–20.

Greenson, R., *The Technique and Practice of Psychoanalysis* (Connecticut: International Universities Press, 1967).

Hougaard, E., 'Dodo-kendelsen' i psykoterapiforskningen I, *Non-specificitetsantagelsen* (Agrippa, 1989), p. 85–104.

Jacoby, R,, *The Repression of Psychoanalysis: Otto Fenichel and the Political Freudians* (University of Chicago Press, 1986).

Johnstone, K., *Impro* (New York: Basic Books, 1986).

Knight, R. P., 'The Present Status of Organized Psychoanalysis in the United States', *Journal of the American Psychoanalytic Association*, I (1953), p. 218-19.

Lassen, L. C., *Compliance i almen praksis* (Institut for Almen Medicin, Kobenhavns Universitet, 1989).

Lévi-Strauss, C., *Structural Anthropology: the Sorcerer and His Magic* (New York: Doubleday, 1967).

Lévi-Strauss, C., 'The Effectiveness of Symbols', in Lessa, W., and Vogt, E., eds., *Reader in Comparative Religion* (New York: Harper and Row, 1979).

Lunde, I.M., *Patienters egenvurdering et medicinsk perspektivskift* (FADL, 1990).

Malcolm, J., *Psychoanalysis: the Impossible Profession* (New York: Vintage, 1982).

Masson, J. M., *Final Analysis: the Making and Unmaking of a Psychoanalyst* (New York: Addison-Wesley, 1990).

Noll, P., *Diktate über Sterben und Tod* (Zurich: Pendo Verlag, 1984).

Reik, T., *Thirty Years with Freud* (New York: Farrar and Rinehart, 1940).

Salling, A.-L., *Stimulation af patienters aktivitet og udvikling* (Dansk Sygeplejerad, 1990).

Taussig, M., *Shamanism, Colonialism, and the Wild Man: a Study in Terror and Healing* (University of Chicago Press, 1987).

Taussig, M., 'Violence and Resistance in the Americas: the Legacy of Conquest', *Journal of Historical Sociology*, III (1990) p. 209-24.

Thompson, J., 'Compliance', in Fitzpatrick, R., *et al.*, *The Experience of Illness* (London: Tavistock Publications, 1984).

Dennis Walder

Resituating Fugard:
South African Drama as Witness

The recent work of the South African dramatist Athol Fugard has addressed the present realities of a country undergoing traumatic change. But on whose behalf does it speak today? The common claim of critics has been that his work 'bears witness': but what does this claim amount to in the context of current debates about culture in South Africa? Central to these debates is the contextualizing work which has arisen out of the neo-Marxist emphasis on previously marginalized black dramatic forms: tending to supplant the liberal, universalizing approach which helped promote Fugard, this is fast becoming a new orthodoxy, diminishing his contribution and historic influence alike. In this article, Dennis Walder looks more closely at the European origins among the liberal-left of the idea of 'bearing witness', and considers its continuing potential as taken up by Fugard himself at a turning-point in the development of his plays – the moment from which sprang both *Boesman and Lena* and the collaborative *Sizwe Bansi* and *The Island*. These plays can still be understood to offer a voice to the voiceless – above all to Lena, the 'Hotnot' woman, an outcast among outcasts, who affirms her identity through her body and her language. Dennis Walder, who was born and brought up in South Africa and educated at the Universities of Cape Town and Edinburgh, is now Senior Lecturer in Literature at the Open University: a Dickens scholar, whose *Dickens and Religion* appeared in 1981, he also wrote the first book-length study of *Athol Fugard* (Macmillan, 1984), and is currently editing Fugard's plays for Oxford University Press.

AS SOUTH AFRICA lurches from crisis to crisis in the trauma and confusion of transition to a non-racial democratic state, the playwright Athol Fugard finds himself 'a lot more hopeful', though 'aware of how precarious the moves towards a new dispensation are'. His new hopefulness applies to the theatre in South Africa, too – a theatre unique because 'In no other country is there as direct and electrifying a relationship between an event on the stage and the social and political reality on the streets.' According to Fugard, this relationship will continue to be important since, although the country appears at last to be moving towards real democracy, its characteristic moral tensions and challenges will long continue to exert creative pressure upon its playwrights.[1]

Fugard's own practice as a playwright has from the start of his career reflected a 'direct and electrifying' relationship with social and political reality, although for many years now – at least since the appear-

ance of *Dimetos* in 1975 – a more inward, mythopoeic concern has also been increasingly evident. But his long-term interest in 'bearing witness' to the immediate sufferings of his compatriots – from the early 'township' plays such as *No-Good Friday* (1958) and *Nongogo* (1959) to *Boesman and Lena* (1969) and the 'Statements' plays of 1972-73 – seems under the pressure of recent events to have returned.

Thus, his last play, *My Children! My Africa!* (1989) was a direct response to an event which took place five years before on the streets of a black township in the Eastern Cape – the murder of a schoolmaster by youths who believed him to be a collaborator. John Kani, the former Serpent Player and now artistic director of the Market Theatre, accepted Fugard's invitation to play the betraying and betrayed elderly schoolmaster, Mr. M. Yet if audiences in Johannesburg and Cape Town, London and New York responded favourably to this play, the huge enthusiasm which had greeted, say, 'Master Harold' . . . and the Boys (1982), was lacking; and critical reaction to Fugard's newly direct and relevant turn was, at best, mixed (its immediate predecessor was the parabolic *A Place with the Pigs*).[2]

One reason for this lukewarm reaction appeared to be that although *My Children! My Africa!* demonstrated yet again Fugard's power and authority in response to a contemporary issue – in this case, how far opposition to the dominant ideology can go before it betrays itself – the play's moral and dramatic focus is finally uncertain. Most damaging is its concluding emphasis on Isabel, the young white schoolgirl, and her spiritual yearnings as a source of future deliverance, while her black counterpart Thami leaves for military training abroad – an ending which at the time of the play's opening felt forced, and which now, in the light of changed circumstances (the end of the armed struggle and the return of exiles), seems irrelevant. But is it?

Soliloquy as 'Voice of the Suppressed'

Whether a theatre tied so closely to its moment of production can survive that moment is always a question, and this is nowhere so obvious as in South Africa, precisely because of the uniquely close relationship between the 'event on the stage' and 'the social and political reality on the streets'. But even in *My Children! My Africa!* the result is more complex than Fugard's mimetic emphasis would suggest – as the play's central, highly artificial structuring device of parallel soliloquies confirms.

Soliloquy has always been important in Fugard's theatrical practice – not only as a familiar convention of European theatre for exploring memory or for other kinds of subjective extension (as in *The Blood Knot*), but also as a means of direct address (Sizwe's 'Am I not a man' speech to the audience in *Sizwe Bansi*) or communal rallying cry ('Nyana we Sizwe!' in *The Island*). The monologues in *My Children! My Africa!* represent a further development of this theatrical device, a recognition of and also a response to the contemporary cultural phenomenon of union rallies, mass funerals, and other (formerly illegal) gatherings in South Africa, a rising chorus of voices from the politically unempowered – 'the public speech as testimony', as Stephen Gray called it at the time of the first performances.[3]

Monologue or soliloquy in Fugard's work has long served as the voice of the suppressed, the silenced, and *My Children! My Africa!* provides a forceful medium for the new voice of township youth. This touches on the fundamental, validating motive of Fugard's career as a playwright, and that aspect of his work which may help it survive beyond the formative moments of its origins: its drive to bear witness, through providing a voice for the voiceless. Yet ending *My Children! My Africa!* with the white girl's claim on the future prompts the question: how far does the fact of it being the white liberal playwright Fugard who provides this voice affect what it says? Further, now that so many of the voiceless are speaking for themselves, who is Fugard to try and speak on their behalf? And in the context of multiracial audiences – at the Market and Baxter Theatres, if not yet more widely – whom does he address?

Another way of putting this would be to say that although *My Children! My Africa!* may connect with the 'reality' of the streets in terms of the conflict between militant black youth and the elderly black collaborator, the question is – what 'reality' does it address through mediating Fugard's concern with the redemptive potential for whites of acknowledging the suffering for others implicit in their own privileged position? Does Fugard's play finally limit itself to addressing a white liberal constituency at home and abroad? And if so, is it sufficient of an achievement to make that audience hear the young black township activists who have, as much if not more than any single identifiable group within South Africa, paid for as well as initiated change? What kind of witness does this imply?

At the structural centre of the play (Act I, Scene vi) Thami addresses the audience in an extended monologue justifying his and his fellows' resistance to education: it is a trap from which they are escaping to the other school of

the streets, the funeral parlours of our location . . . anywhere the people meet and whisper names we have been told to forget, the dates of events they try to tell us never happened and the speeches they try to say were never made . . . . (Faber edn., p. 42-3)

He ends by climbing onto the school bench with raised fist: 'AMANDLA'. This is unquestionably powerful in word and act. But it does not stand alone: it is framed and thus qualified by Mr. M's and the white schoolgirl Isabel's monologues: the self-confessed 'old-fashioned traditionalist' who believes in the final 'power of the word' and who is determined to fight against 'boycotts and arson, mob violence and lawlessness' (p. 20, 51, 58), and the 'average young white South African' who has 'discovered a new world' in the township, who also resists the boycotts and violence (and similarly runs them indiscriminately together as forms of protest), and who promises in the end to make her life 'useful' in the way Mr. M's was (p. 14, 68). The play's dramatic structure guarantees some weight to all three voices – even the naive young woman's, arguably a potential challenge to the masculinist discourses of black radicalism as well as of traditional African patriarchy.

A New, Neo-Marxist Orthodoxy

This highlights the most important thing about *My Children! My Africa!* – it offers a contestation of values, a debate, not simply an expression of one viewpoint. On one level this is quite obvious, since the debate format dominates its structure. This may well appear to outsiders, to those unfamiliar with the immediate (and historic) realities of the country, a somewhat trite theatrical device; yet, like Fugard's use of soliloquy, it goes beyond its origins, at least registering a situation in which for the first time there is the beginning of an open discussion about fundamental issues across formerly rigid class, race, and gender divides.

This is one immensely potent feature of the present moment of painful transition in South Africa: the sound of many voices, previously suppressed or unheard, speaking out and arguing with each other. Among other matters of concern, a wide-ranging debate on culture has arisen, and as part of that debate, a new questioning of the role and function of education – the ostensible subject of *My Children! My Africa!*[4]

How far this new questioning involves drama remains to be seen; although Fugard's remarks alone suggest it has begun. And even before his speech, there had appeared Martin Orkin's book *Drama and the South African State* (1991), an ambitious attempt to resituate South African theatrical history. Orkin's work, completed before the De Klerk reformist initiative began with Mandela's release in February 1990, contains a four-page Postscript, dated March 1990, which concludes:

In what must be a hopeful, even thrilling, but dangerously unpredictable period, many of the plays discussed in this book still bear witness, as they always will, to that which has for so long blighted this country. But, as important, in their very determination to address directly, represent or fictively interact with the social order from which they come, they provide a glimpse of and prepare for a democratic South Africa. (p. 252)

Orkin does not specify which plays might 'still bear witness, as they always will', much less those which in their determined but varied relations with the social order might 'provide a glimpse of and prepare for' the hoped-for future. Does he have Fugard's work in mind? It would appear not, since he characterizes Fugard as a 'dissident member of the ruling class', whose work is disabled by the 'construction of subjectivity primarily in terms of liberal and existentialist discourse' (p. 146-7) – a 'construction' confirmed by 'traditionalist', 'colonialist', and/or 'assimilationist' discourse at home and abroad.

This dismissive account is modified by the admission that *The Blood Knot* and *Boesman and Lena* show 'interiority itself' as partly the product of 'material and social pressures' (p. 130). But Fugard's uniquely important work with the Serpent Players is minimized, and his crucial, innovatory, and influential incorporation of Brecht and Grotowski within the discourses of South African dramaturgy is drastically underplayed. Orkin's aim is, instead, to foreground the black urban drama tradition.

While there is no question that the drama of, say, Herbert Dhlomo in the 'twenties and 'thirties or the more recent work of Gibson Kente (compromised as some of it may be) should feature in any discussion of drama in South Africa, it is hard to guess which of their works might survive the Marxist-structuralist artillery Orkin brings to bear on Fugard, or which might begin to fulfil his concluding criteria.

Orkin deserves high praise for his attempt to remap the theatrical ground in South Africa in terms of European cultural materialism, while drawing on the latest local theatre scholarship. But by concluding with the familiar, unexamined criteria of the artwork as enduring witness and/or reflection of social reality, his book ends up locked in an insufficiently questioning, pre-reform posture.

For a start, it is surely time to question the familiar notion of 'bearing witness', with which he concludes – apparently unaware that it derives from that same 'liberal and existentialist discourse' he wants his readers to disavow. As long as the terms of analysis of the relationship between culture and society are taken over too easily from what has become a familiar metropolitan orthodoxy of dissent, such inconsistencies are likely to continue, obstructing the new and more open debate the changing times demand.

The rise of a neo-Marxist orthodoxy in opposition to the traditional liberal establishment in (predominantly white) academic circles in South Africa lies behind Orkin's work, as it does behind most of the important theatrical scholarship and criticism to emerge from the country in the last decade. The time is overdue for its limitations to be acknowledged, and for discussion to move forward.

One result of the growing debate about culture in South Africa has been a discernible opening up of a space between the two established critical positions – on the one hand the familiar liberal humanist position, long tainted by acceptance of the status quo, yet clinging to important notions of the value and autonomy of specific cultural forms; and on the other this more recent, Marxist-structuralist approach, functional in general and reductive in detail, yet politically informed and theoretically progressive.

Fugard's work may well have been too easily incorporated, its gaps filled, its silences smothered, by that old liberal embrace. On the other hand, as Orkin's book demonstrates, it has come to be too easily dismissed in the pursuit of alternative cultural practices. The rewriting of history, including cultural history, which Fugard's student Thami demands in *My Children! My Africa!* is proceeding apace; but this should mean more than the replacement of one monolithic version of what has happened with another. If the relationship between 'texts' and other signifying practices has to be renegotiated, this should be towards a wider, not narrower range of interpretations of the relationship between culture and society.

The Patriarchal Tradition

Insofar as Fugard's work may be resituated in relation to a changing South Africa, it may have the potential not only to 'bear witness' , but also to offer important new awarenesses – of the past, the present, and (who knows?) the future. And to show this requires a more questioning approach to his work, as well as the work of those many others whose voices have not been heard.

This means, amongst other things, interrogating such catch-all, validating phrases – not just because so many critics and commentators (myself included) have followed Fugard in applying it as a legitimating term; but also because of its continuing, wider provenance, not just in South Africa.

Many writers and artists today feel a special imperative when confronted by the extreme conditions of the twentieth century, by the catastrophes of recent history. One way of describing this imperative has been to say that they feel impelled in some sense to 'bear witness' to the events of their time. In the face of suffering so intense or widespread that it seems to defeat the possibility of art, the idea of bearing witness offers something to cling to across the boundaries of class, race, gender, and nation state – a criterion it is possible to admit as specifically human, without falling into facile universalism.

The phrase has a long history in the cultural formation of the West, but appears to have found new life in the post-colonial era, and not only in the West, as a means of providing some kind of focus within the swirling uncertainties of contested discourse generated by the large, historic changes which everyone can sense happening today. Thus the Mexican poet and essayist, Octavio Paz, has remarked of the writings of Solzhenitsyn that 'If history is the testing ground' he 'has passed the test'.

His example is not intellectual or political or even, in the normal sense of the word, moral. We have to use an even older word, a word which still retains a religious overtone – a hint of death and sacrifice: *witness*. In a century of false testimonies, a writer becomes a witness to man.[5]

And to woman? In this context, how can we forget, for example, Anna Akhmatova's 'Requiem', bearing witness to the long lines of mothers, wives, sisters, and daughters who stood outside Stalin's prisons? Or the Argentinian women who still stand in the main square of post-Galtieri Buenos Aires? Paz has his own agenda: he is responding to a set of writings which call into question one familiar tyranny and by extension a kind of tyranny specific to our time. He is calling for recognition of what has been achieved, and may yet be achieved, by writers who engage with the particular horrors of their societies, attempting also to speak out to the future. Nevertheless, he writes from a specific position within the competing and interlocking discourses of the post-colonial era – one which implicitly obscures or devalues the testimony of women.

As Jane Miller has pointed out, it is a mistake to assume too readily that post-colonial discourses share the same agenda as feminist discourses.[6] One reason for Paz's deletion of women may lie precisely in that crucial 'overtone' acknowledged in the 'older word': religion. The idea of witness in the West derives from the patriarchal Christian discourse.

The original Greek word for witness as it appears in the Christian gospels is *martus*, hence 'martyr'. The legal notion of witnessing the truth of a matter through having oneself seen the action or heard the words spoken was transformed by its use for those who had witnessed Christ's life and resurrection – that is, the apostles. Subsequently those who had undergone hardship for the faith, even suffered death for their belief, came to have the more specialized term reserved for themselves. The 'hint' of death and sacrifice retained by 'witness' is an ineradicable trace of its origins in the Christian tradition of martyrdom.

Separating Writer and Text

Given this originating history, we can think of the kind of witness potentially offered by drama as something special, *sui generis*: since drama is a way of using the body itself as public testimony – the body of the actor/actress, and sometimes, as in Fugard's own practice, the writer/director's body. That transient, living presence which is unique to theatrical production itself provides the continuing potential for offering a witness to the experience, the suffering, of others. How, then, has Fugard's own work offered to 'bear witness'?

In the first place, the answer – any answer – to the question has to take into account the material fact that the work, the 'texts', are separable from the playwright. It is more than merely a matter of post-Barthesian awareness to problematize the automatic fusing of the identity of the individual writer with the works s/he has been involved in at various and different levels of actual practice.

Some of these works – as Fugard himself freely confesses but as reviewers, critics and publishers commonly overlook – cannot without distortion be claimed as simply 'his'. Their ownership is itself a question. The most obvious examples might appear to be the early 'township' dramas, which were the first published plays with Fugard's name attached to them, *No-Good Friday* and *Nongogo*. These plays were derived directly from the white playwright's encounters with black people (such as Zakes Mokae and Lewis Nkosi) and the township subculture of the multiracial ghetto Sophiatown in the late 'fifties; and they have already been thoroughly analyzed as an expression of the liberal multiracialism of certain white and black intellectuals of the time by Robert Kavanagh.[7]

There may not be very much more to be said about them, although they represent an historic moment in the 'discovery' by a larger public of the creative, imaginative, and intellectual potential of black urban performance traditions – traditions which, again, have been extensively and persuasively explored, for example in David Coplan's *In Township Tonight!* (1985).

More usefully provoking in this context might be an account of *The Blood Knot*, which established Fugard's success at home and abroad, and which was also derived from collaborative effort to an extent which continues to be overlooked – overlooked because of the tendency of critics and 'culture-brokers' such as Kavanagh or Coplan, or (more recently) Orkin and Ian Steadman, to adopt a narrowly functional, instrumental version of Gramsci's cultural theory (mediated by Raymond Williams) as a way of admitting black urban theatre into academic discourse and – the hope continues to be – to provide a blueprint for using theatre to advance 'the struggle'.[8]

Nobody can deny that this approach has during the last decade promoted a much greater awareness of the cultural and political contribution, actual or potential, of black urban theatre; but it has simultaneously distorted cultural history, most obviously in this context by diminishing and obscuring the subversive, transforming achievement of the work associated with Fugard – including *Blood Knot*, but also *Boesman and Lena* (which rarely gets more than a mention now, although Orkin is an exception); and, most strikingly, by the 'Statements' plays. 'Most strikingly', because it was the successful collaborative practice of Fugard, Kani, and Ntshona – itself derived from the whole Serpent Players project – which ensured not just international recognition for them but also, as Mongane Wally Serote for one has acknowledged, showed the way to local theatre workers under the sway of the Black Consciousness movement, who went on to produce such remarkable 'township' plays as *Egoli, Hungry Earth, Woza Albert, Bopha, You Have Struck a Rock*, and the rest.[9]

The Instability of Meaning

The meanings of the works associated with Fugard as they continue to be produced are less stable than is assumed even by South African neo-Marxists – not just because instability of meaning characterizes drama in general, as a series of performances at particular times and places, but also because, in the particular case of Fugard, it is an explicit part of his working practice and conscious aesthetics – which consistently privilege the performers, the performing moments, and their history over the printed text.

Indeed, the playwright has felt obliged to admit that instability into the printed version. The revised version of what he retitled simply *Blood Knot*, as a signal of this revision, has long given the role of the darker-skinned, apparently dependent black brother Zach much more force and prominence than in its first performed and published versions, while the guilty, self-pitying reflections of the whiter brother Morris were dropped so as further to expose the subversive elements in the tormented dependency relationship between the two men – and, I would suggest, to register the growing Black Consciousness movement.

It was no mere coincidence that this development was embodied in a 'finalized' new text by means of a production featuring Fugard himself and his original partner and co-creator, Zakes Mokae, in New York – where Mokae was living in exile. Their joint presence ensured that Mokae's contribution was continuing, as well as historical, and not merely allowed to become (or remain) invisible within the familiar processes of cultural production.

Nevertheless, *Blood Knot* as it now survives in print has severe limitations, and it is arguable that its remaining importance is 'historical', in the sense that it was the appearance of this play, and especially of Zakes Mokae as co-actor and collaborator in it, in the New Brighton township outside Port Elizabeth in March 1962 which led to the request from a group of amateur drama enthusiasts from the township – 'the old, old request' as Fugard confided to his notebooks at the time: 'actually it is hunger. A desperate hunger for meaningful activity – to do something that would make the hell of their daily existence meaningful'.[10]

Fugard, exhausted from *The Blood Knot* tour, none the less felt he could not refuse, and so, under his experienced direction, the group – a clerk, two teachers, a bus driver, and domestic servants – embarked upon a series of adaptations of 'classical' European works running from Machiavelli to Brecht, and from Sophocles to Büchner.[11]

White Guilt and White Activism

Kavanagh has suggested that Fugard's motives in thus joining what was to become a uniquely creative and influential collaborative venture across the racial divide are questionable. He quotes Steve Biko asking: 'How many white people fighting for their version of a change in South Africa are really motivated by genuine concern and not by guilt?'[12] He is apparently unaware that this could be taken to reflect upon himself as much, if not more than, Fugard: but what really matters is less Biko's emphasis upon white guilt than his emphasis upon white activists fighting for *their version* of change.

In other words, it is the ideological motivation that matters rather than individual psychology, although of course the latter participates in and is shaped by the former. I have no doubt that Fugard's motives, like those of many people in South Africa and abroad – some of whom are not directly affected by apartheid – involve guilt; but does this matter if what they are prompted to do deeply affects the consciousness of victims and oppressors, and all those not so easily categorized?

The question then becomes: how far, if at all, has Fugard's contribution as a playwright done all or any of this? And what are the terms, what is the context in which this contribution is defined? As I have been trying to suggest, the answer is not as simple as has come to be assumed under the pressures of the 'seventies and 'eighties, especially by white radical academics trying to respond to the Black Consciousness Movement in a time of increasing violence and polarization of viewpoints.

Of course it is important in the postcolonial world to seek to reinstate the marginalized; but this means more than simply the replacing of one dominant tradition by another – even supposing that this were as simple as is presumed. It means questioning the terms which have recently come to dominate critical and theoretical discussion, questioning their own historical and cultural baggage. If the Fugardian *oeuvre* appears to South African cultural materialists to be too readily incorporated into the canonized tradition, this is at least partly the product of their own limited notions of the canonizing process – commonly anathematized in simplistic terms as 'Leavisite'.

So it may be helpful, as the country's social, political, and ideological formations shift into a new phase, to begin formulating a new answer, rather than reiterating familiar oppositions. One way of doing this in relation to the Fugardian 'intervention' is to resituate that phrase, which has commonly stood as a kind of shorthand for the complex, contradictory impulses which have shaped the plays and their reception – 'bearing witness' – and yet which is not transparent, which comes with its own, hitherto unexamined historical and ideological weight.

It's instructive, and an aid to objectivity, to consider the origins of the phrase within a framework derived from a different but analogous extreme historical moment: the holocaust – a period of racial genocide and imprisonment, war, occupation, and resistance, which was succeeded by a massive attempt at social, political, and cultural reconstruction.

The Nature of 'Bearing Witness'

In one of Primo Levi's books about the twenty months he spent in the Nazis' hands, *If This is a Man* (1958), he recalled the beginning of his internment, when even the urge to wash himself had disappeared. 'Why should I wash?' he asked a fellow internee. 'Would I live a day, an hour longer? . . . We will all die, we are about to die.' But the other man administered a 'complete lesson' to him, 'not forgotten either then or later':

that precisely because the Lager was a great machine to reduce us to beasts, we must not become beasts; that even in this place one can survive, and therefore one must want to survive, to tell the story, to bear witness.[13]

Levi survived to tell the story, to bear witness: the man who taught him the lesson did not. Much later, Levi went on to argue that 'we, the survivors, are not the true witnesses': only those who did not survive the concentration camps could truly bear witness to what had happened in them, since only they had fully experienced the ultimate horror, the gas chambers.[14]

The ultimate horror in South Africa has been taking place year after year on death row in Pretoria Central Prison, identified as such by certain writers, including on the white radical side Hugh Lewin, and on the black radical side Lewis Nkosi. And yet, obviously, for all that such writers have experienced, within and outside their country, none of them has, or could have had, the experiences of the condemned men singing on their way to the gallows.[15]

The point is this: if, in an extreme situation, a situation of degradation, brutality,

and even death, it is important to bear witness, who is it that can or should bear witness? And on whose behalf? Do the victims speak for themselves? And if they cannot, who can legitimately speak for them? Which voices are heard, and which have been silenced? And does the passage of time and history change the answers? These are some the questions which underlie the claim to 'bear witness'.

What, then, does Fugard's claim to bear witness amount to, in the changing South African context? To begin to answer the questions posed by Levi's writings we must be precise about when and in what way the claim has been made, and how it has been received: and the personal and historical moment of its inception is revealing.

It was in mid-1968, while Fugard was completing *Boesman and Lena*, and simultaneously turning over the ideas which were eventually to find their expression in the 'Statements' plays, that he confided to his notebooks the notion that his 'life's work was possibly just to witness as truthfully as I could, the nameless and destitute (desperate) of this one little corner of the world' (*Notebooks*, August 1968, p. 172). Like many who had opposed the government during the post-Sharpeville crackdown on dissent, if only by trying to clarify its oppressive nature and work across racial boundaries, Fugard had been identified as a danger, his passport taken away and himself, his family and friends made subject to surveillance.

Isolated, unable to leave the country except on a one-way exit permit, beset with doubts about the resurgence of the international playwrights' boycott, his sources of consolation at the time, apart from his wife and daughter, were threefold. Firstly, *Boesman and Lena*, the play he was writing about the dispossessed 'coloured' and black people he had observed scrabbling for a living on the desolate Swartkops mudflats outside Port Elizabeth; secondly, the experimental workshop he had been engaged in since 1963 with the New Brighton 'township' group, Serpent Players, including most recently John Kani, Winston Ntshona, and a man just released from Robben Island,

Norman Ntshinga, whose experiences were to become directly embodied in *Sizwe Bansi* and *The Island*; and thirdly, the writings of Albert Camus, with whom he was long familiar, but rereading whose *Carnets* made him feel he was 'finding, and for the first time, a man speaking my own language' (*Notebooks*, August 1968, p. 94).

Camus' *Carnets* begin with the words, 'I must bear witness. When I see things clearly, I have only one thing to say. It is in this life of poverty, among these vain or humble people, that I have most certainly touched what I feel is the true meaning of life'.[16] By echoing Camus' words, by making them his own, Fugard found a way of surviving the intense pressures upon him.

The Antecedents of Authentication

What Fugard is doing is in effect calling upon the Western European, Christian-humanist cultural tradition to authenticate his work. What he does not, perhaps cannot, take into account is that this tradition was already half incorporated into a colonial response through the white Algerian Camus' adoption of it. Camus was taking up the same tradition, consciously secularized, which can be found most stirringly expressed in Jean-Paul Sartre's *What is Literature?* (1948), and which also found its way into Primo Levi's work.

In other words, the metropolitan left-wing writer's response to the historical moment of European liberation from war, occupation, and resistance was mediated for Fugard's incorporation by a white, liberal colonial writer whose own colonial country was to become engaged in a struggle for liberation – and one which, for all his sympathy with the Arab underclass, Camus could not finally accept.

What is striking, if we follow this thread, is how, in the colonial appropriation of the idea of bearing witness, something gets lost, or is it excluded, *silenced*? When Sartre talks of bearing witness – and he uses the same phrase throughout *What is Literature?* – he has in mind an 'appeal' which the writer thereby addresses to two publics simul-taneously: to his own (bourgeois) class, it is 'an incitement to revolt . . . to the ruling class [it is] an invitation to lucidity, to critical self-examination, to the giving up of its privileges'.

Sartre provides two examples: Rousseau, whose writings about human freedom *'bore witness'* before the nobility, and at the same time invited the commoners to 'become conscious of themselves. It was not only the taking of the Bastille which his writings . . . were preparing at long range; it was also the night of August the fourth':[17] that is, the night in 1789 when the National Assembly renounced feudal privileges in an attempt to keep the revolution going on their terms (the parallel with the South African government in 1991 is irresistible).

Sartre's second example is equally illuminating. If Rousseau's work can be seen by bearing witness both to make his own class conscious of themselves, and to appeal to the aristocracy to give up their privileges, thereby anticipating the bourgeois revolution of 1789, the same can be said of the work of the black American Richard Wright 'when he writes for both enlightened negroes and whites'.[18] There is, in other words, a *fracture*, along race as well as class lines, at the heart of Wright's public: as Sartre puts it elsewhere, the words Wright 'puts on paper have not the same context for whites as for negroes', since

whatever the goodwill of the white readers may be, for a negro author they represent the *Other*. . . . It is only from without that he conceives their proud security and that tranquil certainty, common to all white Aryans, that the world is white and that they own it. The words he puts down on paper have not the same context for whites as for negroes . . . [whereas for his own people] in trying to become clear about his own situation, he clarifies theirs for them. . . . And when he speaks to [the whites], it is a matter of implicating them and making them take stock of their responsibilities.[19]

As this implies, in words closely applicable to black and white South African writers today, their fractured audience involves them in saying different things to different people, whatever may be their own views or motives. As Sartre says, the words are the same, but the context is not. And yet this isn't necessarily a disadvantage. It is a question, once again – as the examples of Rousseau and Wright indicate – of who is speaking, on whose behalf, to whom, and at what historical moment.

The Silenced Testimony?

Yet all the critics – in South Africa and abroad – have simply accepted Fugard's claim to 'bear witness' at face value, thereby effectively excluding the radical, indeed revolutionary possibilities, in both class and race terms, which since Sartre at any rate have come to overlay its original Christian humanist meanings. Stephen Gray observed some time ago that 'the majority of Fugard scholars and reviewers and critics come from the liberal humanist camp' – white liberal humanist camp might be more accurate. Gray appeared to exclude himself from this camp by going on to point out that such critics commonly prefer their 'considerations of the human condition ultimately to be non-political', whereas Fugard's 'Questioning, in the context of the apartheid society into which [he] was born and in which he chooses to continue to work, can also be a political act'.[20]

'Can also be'? Yes, but is it? Gray himself did not stay to answer, and the exclusion from his anthology of all but generally uncritical, not to say laudatory views, suggested that his own position was closer to the liberal humanists than he was willing or able to admit. But it is also a fact that, apart from an article by Hilary Seymour in *Race and Class* challenging what she perceived to be the liberal inadequacies of *Sizwe Bansi is Dead*,[21] no serious response from outside the liberal humanist camp had appeared by the time Gray compiled his anthology.

This is no longer the case, as I indicated earlier in my remarks about the more recent Marxist-structuralist criticism of Orkin, Kavanagh, Steadman, and Coplan. Of course the liberal viewpoint continues in play – whether in the academic or professional arena inhabited by, for example, Russell Vandenbroucke's massive attempt to claim the moral high ground, *Truths the Hand Can Touch: the Theatre of Athol Fugard* (1985), which endorses throughout Fugard's 'metaphysical', 'universal' and 'transcendent' concerns, or in the more popular and influential world of newspapers and magazines such as *Time*, which on 18 April 1988 endorsed Fugard's implicit claim for worldwide attention in similar terms, to the continuing delight of the South African liberal press.

The move to promote a distinctive alternative critical tradition, consciously taking into account historical and ideological factors, would seem in this context to be just what is needed. Perhaps it was. But the form it has taken has come to block the potential for the continuing testimony of *Sizwe Bansi* or *The Island*, or indeed *Boesman and Lena* – a testimony yet unheard in them, silenced, yet still asking for recognition.

The nearest Fugard himself has approached offering a witness to the extreme of suffering in South Africa appears to lie in his part in the collaborative venture which resulted in *The Island*. The play does not encompass Pretoria Central; but it none the less takes in the 'living death' of perpetual imprisonment in the maximum security prison on the island. And it had its immediate origins at that key moment in Fugard's career in 1968 when he first enunciated his idea of 'bearing witness' to the experiences of others.

Those 'others' were in the event the Serpent Players, whose experiences under harassment, arrest, and imprisonment he felt he couldn't watch without witnessing. Ironically, the distancing from the actual experience which his race and position made unavoidable for him was to some extent shared by the co-creators of the play, John Kani and Winston Ntshona, who, although much more likely to share that experience, did not in practice do so. Kani's more politically active brother had been imprisoned, but it was the released players Welcome Duru and Norman Ntshinga who initially bore witness, because they (especially Ntshinga) told Fugard and the remaining Players the story of what happened to them on Robben Island – including making up stories and putting on 'shows' to articulate their feelings, and help them, up to a point, to survive: but Ntshinga, for one, has never fully recovered.

The Function of 'Protest Plays'

All three co-creators of *The Island* may be said to have borne witness by speaking out on behalf of the silenced and in their varied relations to them at that moment of their oppression. It is a moment that has passed. Does this mean that their work no longer bears witness? The obvious point to be made emerges when you consider the subsequent production history of this joint work in relation to the larger history of events in the country. When, for example, *The Island* was revived with its original cast and co-devisers from Serpent Players, John Kani and Winston Ntshona, at the Baxter Theatre in Cape Town in 1985, the production was accompanied by the following programme note:

We, John Kani and Winston Ntshona, declare every single performance of this play, *The Island*, as an endorsement of the local and international call for the immediate release of Mr. Nelson Mandela and all political prisoners and detainees. We earnestly hope that this call will receive the support of all well-meaning South Africans.[22]

Nothing could more clearly indicate how the two black co-creators had come to view their performances in the play, and, further, how they appealed to their racially fractured yet multiracial audiences to do so, too – as the 'endorsement' of a specific protest, a call for specific political action on behalf of those 'political prisoners and detainees'. But equally, today nothing could more clearly indicate how that level of the play's witness has become almost irrelevant. (I say 'almost' irrelevant, since although Nelson Mandela *has* been released, as well as many other political prisoners and detainees, some still remain imprisoned around the country, and it isn't long ago that a hunger strike invol-

ving some three hundred prisoners on Robben Island itself drew attention to their continuing plight – a strike withdrawn after Mandela intervened.)

And yet, of course, the extent to which this play, and the other so-called 'Statements' plays, testify directly to the effects of well-known apartheid laws: the pass laws in *Sizwe Bansi*, the Immorality Act in *Statements after an Arrest under the Immorality Act*, and in *The Island* the whole panoply of laws banning the opposition movements – the ANC, the PAC, and the South African Communist Party, not to mention anybody whom the Minister could call a Communist for opposing the governing regime. The extent to which the plays bear witness to the effects of these laws has now been overtaken by their repeal. That is, of course, inevitable, and it means that insofar as the theatre functions as an 'arm of the struggle' it is bound to be overtaken by events in the long if not the short term.

This is not to say that protest theatre, or didactic theatre, or agitprop as it is sometimes dismissively labelled, cannot play a vital role, becoming at its best a source of immediate if not continuing dissent and resistance towards unjust political circumstances. Most of the protest theatre in South Africa since the 'seventies has done just that. As such, it has at the least a historical weight that cannot be ignored.

But, as more and more black South African writers and theatre workers from Njabulo Ndebele to Matsemela Manaka have come to acknowledge, protest writing is severely limited in what it can offer its different audiences – all too often, no more than the opportunity of being patronized by the powerful at home and abroad, and of having your powerlessness confirmed. In so far as black theatre 'keeps on reacting to white domination . . . protesting white oppression', it merely shows that the system still 'controls what we think'.[23]

Such theatre is not just tied to the time and place of its original production, but *locked* to it by its lack of complexity, of ambiguity of image – in short that crucial element of autonomy, of *relative* autonomy, which allows cultural productions to survive their time and place, and exert a transforming pressure upon other times and places. How? By witnessing to what Ngugi wa Thiong'o describes as all those 'ordinary men and women hungering and living in rooms without lights' throughout the Third World.[24] All these South Africans, from Fugard to Manaka, seem to agree.

Whose Commitment?

Can any of the work with which Fugard has been associated still be said to do this? The answer depends upon the kind of testimony we can now discover in it. His present position, as revealed in his most recent practice and utterance, suggests a drive towards opening up further space for other voices, while striving to testify to the dilemmas which remain.

The psychopathology of the white liberal consciousness explored in *Dimetos* or *A Place with the Pigs*, strangely poignant as these semi-allegoric pieces now seem, is of less continuing interest than those past plays which, as John Kani has been saying, 'gave back to the people their voices'.[25] These are the works which contributed to the upsurge of previously suppressed voices we can all hear in South Africa today, and which may continue to exert that power, whatever the limits of Fugard's personal politics.

This might well lead us to resituate all Fugard's collaborative work, including his earliest Sophiatown plays and *The Blood Knot/Blood Knot*, as well as such fugitive productions as *The Coat*.[26] But Kani was in fact referring to the two 'Statements' plays on which he had worked, and which still count as the first to reveal to a larger public what the remarkable blend of creative talent and responsiveness to the everyday pain of their fellow black South Africans could produce in the theatre.

The images brought to Fugard, Ntshona, and Kani by their friends, relations, and collaborators, which they worked on with an ever-accumulating sense of the urgency and relevance of the smallest detail, produced that complex web of monologues which deliberately called out the voices of the silenced others, hence bearing witness to their experience – as those others recognized, for example in the first public performance of *Sizwe Bansi* in the Players' own New Brighton on 23 August 1974, two years after its initial exposure before Cape Town liberals.

This performance was allowed to proceed in the first instance (although the Security Police were present, outside St Stephen's Hall) because of the overseas publicity already generated by the play and its co-creators/performers. As Fugard noted, it was one thing 'to try to educate a comfortable white audience into what the hated Reference Book means to a black man. . . . [It is] something else to confront, and in a sense challenge, an angry black audience with those same realities.'

The anger was there because of a fresh wave of detentions during the build-up of youthful militancy and harsh police reaction which led to the Soweto uprisings of 1976. The evening began with a Brechtian-style announcer (Welcome Duru) introducing Fugard, Kani, and Ntshona, and warning that this was 'straight theatre' – as opposed, that is, to the usual township entertainments. Far from increasing their anger, the production soon had the audience roaring with laughter – until the scene in which passbooks are switched.

A stunned silence at the depiction of this seriously illegal act was followed by a prolonged debate about it among members of the audience. The performance on stage had provoked a political event in the auditorium – the action of the play matched and equalled by the action of the audience, with many people saying for the first time what they felt and thought about their situation. As if to confirm this sense of shared witness, the evening ended with everybody standing up and singing the anthem of the banned ANC, *Nkosi Sikeleli Afrika*.[27]

What this event demonstrated is how the white liberal playwright, isolated by his race and his position within the dominant minority in a fractured, quasi-colonial society, could nevertheless be led by his commit-

John Kani and Winston Ntshona in the passbook scenes from *Sizwe Banzi Is Dead*, directed by Athol Fugard at The Space, Cape Town, October 1972. Photo: Brian Astbury.

ment to bearing witness to participate in a commitment not his own. In initiating and helping to produce plays such as these, Fugard has been taken across the gulfs which the narrow history of race and class prejudice in South Africa has created, to become an actor in the larger history of its transformation.

As he always acknowledges, and we should never forget, this process would have been impossible without the offer of shared witness from his co-creating performers. However, even acknowledging the extent to which Fugard has thereby assisted in the process of giving voice to the voiceless, now that the specific illegality is irrelevant, what kind of testimony do performers continue to offer beyond that?

The most recent performer in *Sizwe Bansi* (Chris Gxalaba) says researching the part led him to ask himself questions he had never asked before about the laws which had controlled his people's lives, while township tours with the play had led him to reach out to new audiences.[28] *Sizwe Bansi* still has the potential to bear witness to the dehumanizing impact of a totalitarian, racist structure – a structure which in its fundamentals continues to exert a profound and corrupting influence upon South African society.

The Irony of 'The Island'

But what about *The Island*? The answer is more complex, and goes back to its history. Anyone remotely familiar with *The Island* will recall that it is about a play within a play, *The Trial and Imprisonment of Antigone*, which is presented to a group of prisoners and warders on Robben Island by two men imprisoned for belonging to the ANC, John and Winston – the actors Kani and Ntshona using their own names, although neither of them had actually been imprisoned.

Once again, it was Fugard's involvement with Serpent Players which led to the group doing a production of Sophocles' classical drama in the 'township' venue of St. Stephen's Church Hall on 27 May 1965 – truly 'a milestone in the development of

theatre in New Brighton', as one of the group, unconscious of the irony, observed the next day.[29] The irony is that there was no hope of such theatre at the time, despite what we now know of the existence of black theatrical traditions: the authorities had set out on a purge of the Eastern Cape, ending in the imprisonment upon Robben Island of two players, including Norman Ntshinga, who took the part of Creon's son Haemon – and who worked up a two-man version of the Greek play for production in prison.

The further irony is that, by resuscitating under extreme conditions the exemplary figures of the highest cultural provenance of Western European tradition, this in itself bore witness to the continuing transformative potential of that tradition, while testifying to the strength of Ntshinga and his people under the worsening circumstances of the late 'sixties.

Ntshinga's subsequent report of the prison production, and other Robben Island activities engaged in by the politicals so as to maintain their sense of dignity and solidarity in the face of humiliation and provocation, so as to wash their faces, in Primo Levi's phrase – this report of prison experiences to Fugard and the Players three years later established the basic elements of the play, refashioning Sophocles' original in order to bring out the prisoners' perspective. Then, after another four years, these were overlain by Ntshona and Kani's hearsay accounts to complete the long testimony of what the imprisoned men had gone through to survive – a testimony which emboldened and inspired many others in the townships to create a dramatic space in which to account for their own sufferings.

But before the final emergence of the 'Statements' works in 1973, another key element, derived from Fugard's more private theatrical development, had to emerge. He had retired into himself under the spell of Peter Brook and Jerzy Grotowski's extreme, experimental, actors' style of theatre to produce *Orestes* in 1971 – a scriptless, nightmare testimony to the 1964 bomb outrage on Johannesburg station, for which a white radical schoolteacher was executed, an instance of the furthest to which white dissent had then gone.

The three (white) performers of this unique and only thrice-performed work included Yvonne Bryceland, whose willingness to extend the boundaries of stage action helped release the creative energies and extreme, physical style of performance – involving nudity, urination, improvised monologues, and other subtextual devices unknown in South Africa – which Fugard later encouraged in the creation of *Sizwe Bansi* and *Die Hodoshe Span* (the original title of *The Island*) for their first private audiences of (predominantly) liberal whites in the Space Theatre. (The Space was founded by Bryceland's partner Brian Astbury in Cape Town in July 1973, precisely in order to provide an outlet for the work that she and Fugard were doing. Both Bryceland and Astbury's roles in this collaborative venture need also to be recalled, as part of its historic witness.)

According to John Kani, the crystallizing moment of *The Island* occurred when 'Athol came up with the idea that there is a place we never talk about, no one can write about, the press cannot talk about, not even white South Africans, free as they are, can talk about.'[30] That is the silence *The Island* helped to break by its presence, which also means by the presence of its black co-creators and performers, whose very appearance in this remarkably physical play was a means of underwriting its demand for expressions of solidarity from the initial audiences of white liberals and later (as with *Sizwe Bansi* but while exploring a more dangerous subject) from black or multiracial audiences at home and abroad.

Witness as Alignment

The two Serpent Players were offering themselves as a sacrifice by proxy for their incarcerated brothers (literally so, in John Kani's case) – an effect further underscored by the fact that it was some time before these early performances could be safely recorded in written form available for other performers and other situations.

Equally important now that the silence has finally been broken are the possibilities of new dimensions in the surviving text of *The Island*, which the voices of others implicitly call into focus – voices such as those of Indres Naidoo (in *Island in Chains*, 1982) and of Michael Dingake (in *My Fight Against Apartheid*, 1987), which testify not only to the comradeship, the strength of black brotherhood expressed in the play's central and repeated cry of *Nyana we Sizwe!*, but also to the extraordinary qualities of leadership, the planned and patiently determined resistance which turned warders into allies, even into friends, and enabled Mandela, Sisulu, and the others to continue to exert a decisive influence beyond the island.

The play's circularity of structure – the two prisoners running off shackled together once again at the end as they arrived at the beginning – expresses endurance under suffering, even passivity, rather than this potential to resist and overcome their oppressors. Not for Fugard, it would seem, any hints of the future and the arrival on South African soil of the new generation of black leaders, ready to take over. This appears to be confirmed by his rueful self-accusation at the time of the play's slow inception of a 'failure of imagination' regarding the future of his country which, he observed to himself in 1968 (*Notebooks*, p. 179), he believed in 'but of which I have no image'.[31]

Does this mean, then, that while offering to 'bear witness' to the experiences and the sufferings of his more politically active black compatriots, the white liberal playwright offered an empowering voice to all those colonized 'others', only simultaneously to withdraw it, by defining the terms in which the 'other' could be expressed?

To some extent, yes. On the other hand, as Primo Levi's remarks remind us, there are limits to any testimony. Fugard's commitment to what he was doing, and his awareness that it involves him in compromise, has been consistent. In those dark days of 1968, as evidence of the government's legacy of 'suffering, of destroyed and wasted lives' grew daily, he reflected on his 'decision to throw in my lot "here and now", to *witness* – what? – if not those people, ideas, values, which left me – the man that I am – with no alternative but to align myself with them'.

But how far 'in this alignment do I stand as an obstacle to the changes which I know will take place sooner or later?' Unable to answer his own question, his instinct tells him to carry on, rather than 'sit in moral paralysis while the days of my one life – my one chance to discover the brotherhood of other men – pass' (*Notebooks*, p. 160-1). Some sense of that 'brotherhood' is what he discovered and helped mediate in his work with Serpent Players, and, most lastingly, in *The Island*.

All the circumstances surrounding the origins, production, and reception of *The Island* suggest something more complex and difficult to tie down than the stereotyping readings of either white liberals or Marxist-structuralists would suggest. And this confirms the possibility of reading the play in terms not so much of agitprop simplicities, but in more varying and ambiguous ways, searching out its continuing potential for witness in the projection of those very ordinary, unheroic, yet particularly human qualities which make for survival under the extreme conditions of colonial and post-colonial oppression with which we are obliged to be familiar.

The Black Woman's Voice

If this makes *The Island* at least seem to fulfil Paz's notion of what 'witness' means, there is the further point that this play also admits a feminist reading. Its defining moment, after all, takes place when Winston dons the classical Greek heroine's gear to express her defiance of the law as she goes to her doom, thereby insisting that the Western European cultural tradition can still be made to bear witness, but with the added resonance that it is *in a woman's voice* that the only finally defiant note of the play is struck. The extreme of humiliation (anticipated by Sizwe/Robert's 'Am I not a man' speech in the preceding play), when Winston throws off the emasculating disguise of the heroine

as his cellmate roars with crude laughter, can now be read as having been transformed into a new possibility of challenge and affirmation, absent from *Sizwe Bansi*.

If this seems improbable, given the dominance of a masculine discourse of opposition in South Africa, there is the striking fact that the Fugard play which arose out of the same personal and historical moment as *The Island* was *Boesman and Lena*. And the climax of that play has the miserable, almost demented Lena find the strength – despite all that she has suffered at the hands of the white man *and* her 'coloured' partner – to sing, to dance, to stamp down upon the mud out of which she has come, and to which she is about to return.

Perhaps the most driving need to be witnessed in extremity is registered here, the need of black women, doubly oppressed by the apartheid system and traditional patriarchy, to have their voices heard. Only very gradually and partially, despite the explicit commitment of the main opposition movement to them, are these voices beginning to sound – in the drama of Fatimah Dike (who worked on two plays at the Space in the 'seventies), in the production of *You Strike the Woman You Strike the Rock* (1986), and, most recently, in the work of actress-storyteller Gcina Mhlophe, whose *Have You Seen Zandile?* (1989) has been predictably marginalized – not by white liberals, but by the neo-Marxists, for whom it offers too 'personal' and subjective a statement.[32]

Yet it is out of the personal and subjective experience that the twin compulsion to tell the truth about and identify with the victims, the underprivileged, is derived; and hence the possibility of artistic, more generalized witness. If this kind of artwork loses its roots in the individual and individualizing imagination, it loses everything. Fugard wrote in his notebook that while watching a Lena-figure on the banks of the Swartkops River, to whom he and his companion were 'merely white men', he felt 'the demand that the truth be told, that I must not bear false witness' in creating her character (*Notebooks*, July 1968, p. 166). A month later, as work on the play proceeded,

Lena (Yvonne Bryceland) tells her story to Outa (Sandy Tubé), who does not understand a word. From the film of *Boesman and Lena*, directed by Ross Devenish for Bluewater Productions, 1973.

he noted that Lena's 'demand that her life be witnessed' expressed more than a 'sense of injustice and abuse', but an 'ontological' insecurity (*Notebooks*, August 1968, p. 173).

This tendency towards the transcendent in Fugard's remarks – apparently confirmed by the reflection that what concerned him was the predicament of Boesman and Lena at a level 'neither political nor social but metaphysical . . . a metaphor of the human condition which revolution or legislation cannot substantially change' (*Notebooks*, p. 173) – has encouraged both the familiar liberal-humanist reading of his work as apolitical, and the Marxist-structuralist reading according to which it is about no more than the 'power of apartheid laws in determining the pattern of individual existence'.[33]

Either way, the work is allowed to retreat into irrelevance, its claim to bear witness limited to the past. But not only does the playtext offer a richer and more ambiguous range of interpretations than these fixed positions allow, so too there is the point that Fugard himself at the time described his *Notebook* remarks as naive and partial. They should be read as a record of specific moments in the creation of what he calls his 'palimpsest', implying dense and multiple layers of meaning rather than any simple concluding judgement or justification (*Notebooks*, p. 169, 172, 174).

We should instead attend to the continuing potential of Lena's plea in Act One, 'I want someone to listen' (which used mistakenly to be printed as 'I was someone to listen,' which, it can now be appreciated, involves a profound misreading of Lena's role).[34] It is a deeply moving irony that the listener who arrives within the play is himself lost in his own suffering, the almost silent, dying black man *Outa* (literally 'old father', commonly used towards an elderly black servant), who cannot understand her words, who may understand her meaning, and yet whose mere presence counts as witness. By a further chilling irony, Boesman later asks Lena to ensure that he isn't blamed for Outa's death – 'Now you want a witness too', she exclaims (Act II, p. 241).

In the Act of Self-Definition

What Fugard has done in trying to bear witness is listen to a voice in the act of self-definition: hoarse and broken, yet, as he noted while thinking of the scene, offering through Lena the woman's 'discovery of value, of herself as having value' (*Notebooks*, Oct. 1967, p. 155). It is less Lena's words, broken and inarticulate as they sound, than her physical presence, her song and her dance as enacted by her first performer Yvonne Bryceland, which clarify this.

Unlike the 'Statements' plays, *Boesman and Lena* was 'totally written first', before Fugard approached Bryceland. Why her? There was nobody available from Lena's submerged class, but in any case Bryceland was a performer born and brought up in the Cape who was able to draw on a lifetime of unconscious absorption of the way of speaking and moving of 'people like Lena'. Fugard (who played Boesman himself at first) inspired her to bring this to conscious embodiment in the precise physicality of her performance and, especially, of dancing at the climactic moment, thereby 'committing myself', as she put it, to expressing Lena.[35]

Lena's 'Hotnot dance', stiff-backed, painful, as she stamps her poor bare feet upon the earth, is also a song, addressed (on p. 233) in the first place to Outa:

Somebody born, somebody buried. We danced them in, we danced them out. . . . Da . . .da . . . da.
Ou blikkie kondens melk
Maak die lewe soet. . . .
Not like your dances. No war-dances for us. They say we were slaves in the old days. Just your feet on the earth and then stamp. Hit it hard! . . . We don't tickle it like the white people . . .

Clap with me. . . .
Korsten had its empties
Swartkops got its bait
Lena's got her bruises
Cause Lena's a Hotnot meid.

'Hotnot' is the abusive term derived from the earliest naming by Dutch settlers of one of the original pre-colonial inhabitants of the country, a people lately (too late for their survival) permitted their own name for themselves as part of the revision of South African history – the Khoikhoi. However, it is unlikely Lena is Khoikhoi, or even Khoisan, the term for both indigenous Cape peoples, including the San or 'Bushmen' – that is, Boesman, as her partner is called, and calls himself.

Rather, Lena is some unknown racial mix, by her very existence denying the long history of the dominant power's attempts to keep people apart – a history going back to the earliest days of Dutch settlement, when van Riebeeck put up the first fences in the Cape to keep out the nomadic aboriginals. Dutch-Afrikaans 'meid' means girl-servant, the lowest of the low.

Thus Lena's living moment dramatically celebrates the specific, historically constituted, racially, linguistically, and culturally mixed identity of the country, in defiance of all the forces for division and hierarchy which have beset its people. And even as we are led to mourn this particular woman's beatings and her lost children, we are confronted by a refusal: to accept the self-destructive violence of her partner, and of a male-dominated society.

What Lena calls 'your dances . . . war-dances' may be a slur on traditional African cultural practices, which include many and varied forms of ritual, narrative, and dramatic activity. But the point is that, as Bessie Head was testifying at the same time – for example in *When Rain Clouds Gather* (1968) and *Maru* (1971) – the illegitimate Hotnot woman has been the outcast among outcasts, the black man's black; and here is a self-proclaimed 'Hotnot meid' affirming her identity through her body and her language – before the black man, before her partner and, finally, before the audience:

predominantly white liberal then, although not *necessarily* so now or in the future.

If *Boesman and Lena* has the potential to do no more than show the limiting impact of apartheid legislation upon the subject (*pace* Orkin), that is a poor hope for its lasting relevance; and if it merely confirms the continuing liberal interpretation which favours its supposed 'metaphysical' claims, it is equally limited. My suggestion is that in the 'post-apartheid' era, the potential in certain of the works associated with Fugard for continuing to bear witness as a complex, intermittent, varying, but transforming and even challenging experience may be felt. If not, what more can we say for the role of drama in the post-colonial dispensation?

Notes and References

1. 'Beware of "cultural commissars" of the left, warns Fugard', in a lecture to Rhodes University staff and students, Grahamstown. See *Cape Argus*, 20 June 1991.

2. See, for example, Thomas J. Arthur, '*My Children! My Africa!* by Athol Fugard', *Theatre Journal*, XLII, No. 2 (1990), p. 246-7; Michael Billington, 'The Word versus the Fist', *The Guardian*, 8 Sept. 1990; Lynne Truss, 'Variations on the Riot Act', *Independent on Sunday*, 9 Sept. 1990.

3. Stephen Gray, '"Between Me and My Country": Fugard's *My Children! My Africa!* at the Market Theatre, Johannesburg', *New Theatre Quarterly*, VI, No. 21 (1990), p. 25-30.

4. For the most important and influential views to date, see Ingrid de Kok and Karen Press, eds., *Spring is Rebellious: Arguments about Cultural Freedom by Albie Sachs and Respondents* (Cape Town: Buchu Books, 1990).

5. Octavio Paz, *On Poets and Others*, trans. M. Schmidt (Manchester: Carcanet, 1987), p. 111-12.

6. See Jane Miller, *Seductions: Studies in Reading and Culture* (Virago, 1990), p. 108-35.

7. See Robert Kavanagh, *Theatre and Cultural Struggle in South Africa* (Zed Books, 1985), especially p. 61-83.

8. See, for example, Ian Steadman, 'Collective Creativity: Theatre for a Post-Apartheid Society', in *Rendering Things Visible: Essays on South African Literary Culture*, ed. Martin Trump (Johannesburg: Ravan Press, 1990), p. 307-21.

9. Mongane Wally Serote, 'Art as Craft and Politics: Theatre', *Arekopeneng*, London, 1986, reprinted in *On the Horizon* (Fordsburg: Congress of South African Writers, 1990), p. 45-7.

10. Athol Fugard, *Notebooks: 1960-1977*, ed. Mary Benson (Johannesburg: Ad Donker, 1983), p. 81, entry for May 1963. All subsequent references are to this edition, silently revised and modified as it has been, unless otherwise specified.

11. See my *Athol Fugard* (Macmillan, 1984), p. 79-82, for a more detailed account.

12. Kavanagh, op. cit., p. 161.

13. Primo Levi, *If This is a Man and The Truce*, trans. Stuart Woolf (Abacus, 1987), p. 47.

14. Primo Levi, *The Drowned and the Saved*, trans. R. Rosenthal (Abacus, 1988), p. 63.

15. Hugh Lewin, *Bandiet: Seven Years in a South African Prison* (Barrie and Jenkins, 1974), p. 134-48; Lewis Nkosi, *Mating Birds* (Constable, 1986), p. 183-4.

16. Albert Camus, 'Notebook 1, May 1935', reprinted in Albert Camus, *Selected Essays and Notebooks*, trans. Philip Thody (Penguin, 1970), p. 235.

17. Jean-Paul Sartre, *What is Literature?*, trans. B. Frechtman (Methuen 1978), p. 80.

18. Ibid., p. 80.

19. Ibid., p. 58-9.

20. Stephen Gray, ed. and Introduction, *Athol Fugard* (Johannesburg: McGraw-Hill, 1982), p. 27.

21. Hilary Seymour, '*Sizwe Bansi is Dead*: a Study of Artistic Ambivalence', *Race and Class*, XXI, No. 3 (1980), p. 273-89.

22. 'An Island of Dreams', *Weekend Argus*, Cape Town, 2 Nov. 1985.

23. See, for example, Njabulo Ndebele, 'The Rediscovery of the Ordinary', *Journal of Southern African Studies*, XII, No. 2 (April 1986), p. 144-57; Matsemela Manaka, 'Human Problems that Come from a Political Situation', interview in *The Drama Review*, XXX, No. 4 (June 1986), p. 48-50.

24. Ngugi wa Thiong'o, Introduction, *Decolonizing the Mind* (James Currey, 1986), p. 3.

25. Personal interview, National Theatre, London, September 1990.

26. Not fugitive for very much longer: see my forthcoming edition of *The Township Plays* (Oxford University Press, 1993).

27. Athol Fugard, 'When Brecht and Sizwe Bansi met in New Brighton', *Observer Review*, 8 August 1982.

28. 'Winner Through Hard Work', *Cape Times*, 8 August 1991.

29. Anonymous, unpublished manuscript, 28 May 1965, Fugard Collection, National English Literary Museum, Grahamstown.

30. Quoted by Russell Vandenbroucke, *Truths the Hand Can Touch: the Theatre of Athol Fugard* (New York: Theatre Communications Group, 1985), p. 126.

31. Compare the earlier, pre-Benson version of this part of the *Notebooks*, reprinted in Athol Fugard, *Boesman and Lena and Other Plays* (Cape Town: Oxford University Press, 1980), p. xxv: 'How do I align myself with a future, a possibility, in which I believe but of which I have no clear image?'

32. M. Orkin, *Drama and the South African State* (Manchester: Manchester University Press; Johannesburg: Witwatersrand University Press, 1991), p. 231.

33. Ibid., p. 141. Again, note that this oft-quoted remark does not appear in Fugard's own first, 1974 version of the *Notebooks*, reprinted in *Boesman and Lena and Other Plays*, op. cit., p. xx-xxv. Was it added later?

34. The correct version of the text may be found in my edition of Athol Fugard, *Selected Plays* (Oxford University Press, 1987), p. 200. Subsequent references are to this edition.

35. Unpublished personal interview with Yvonne Bryceland, London, 21 Sept. 1983.

Gabriella Giannachi and Lizbeth Goodman

Which Freedom? An Overview of Contemporary Bulgarian Theatre

Our 'Update from Eastern Europe', following this article, includes reports from Poland, Czechoslovakia, and Russia – on all of which countries we have published earlier features concerning the problems faced by theatre people in the wake of the disintegration of the Communist bloc. However, the theatre of Bulgaria has been little previously noticed, whether by NTQ or its contemporaries, and requires a more detailed overview. This is now provided by Gabriella Giannachi and Lizbeth Goodman, who visited the country in October 1991, interviewing a wide range of people working in its theatres and seeing a selection of productions in which they were involved. Gabriella Giannachi is a graduate student based at Trinity Hall, Cambridge, and Lizbeth Goodman is Lecturer in Literature at the Open University, whose series of feminist theatres interviews has been published in earlier issues of NTQ.

IT IS PROBABLY not a coincidence that writers of articles on Eastern Europe often feel the need to add a question mark to their titles. As Danilo Manera wrote in his article, 'Bulgaria: How to Turn the Page?' ('Bulgaria: Voltar Pagina, Come?', in *Linea d'Ombra*, No. 66, December 1991), the crisis which Bulgaria has gone through in the last three years is among the most serious in the country's history, and its cultural isolation has been further aggravated by the recent disintegration and civil war in Yugoslavia.

In economic terms, the scarcity of food and particularly of fruit and vegetables, the shortage of petrol, and the runaway rates of inflation have transformed Bulgaria into a wasteland of sorts. Sofia resembles a ghost town, the streets largely deserted during the day and completely dark at night because the government – in order to save energy – fuels street lights only in certain areas.

We went to Bulgaria as researchers, eager to learn about the theatre of a country at the far edge of Europe. We were surprised by what we found: not only in the theatres, but in the streets, and in the words of the many people we met and spoke with. We found, first and foremost, a spirit of uncertainty – a fear that the theatre and cultural life in general might not be able to recover from

the radical changes of the past few years. As academic researchers, we sought an objective critical perspective from which we could examine and write about Bulgarian culture and the theatre – yet we could not ignore the state of the economy. We found Bulgaria in a state of economic flux, and it seemed to us that to be silent about the gravity of the situation would be to share in a conspiracy of silence, and thereby a certain responsibility for the current crisis.

It is not surprising that the theatre in Bulgaria has been affected by the shift from a communist to a socialist regime. Similar situations have been experienced by other Eastern European countries. The theatre was the focus of government attention during the years of censorship, and was therefore 'liberated' by the significant changes which came with its lifting.

In Bulgaria, the theatre was the only mass medium which could at least partially avoid censorship. It is precisely because of this that the theatre succeeded in attracting large audiences of extremely diverse generations, professional groups, and cultural backgrounds. Now, after a period of stasis following the revolution, many people, especially the young, are returning to the theatre, this time with an extremely complex question: once freedom of speech is gained, what can be done with it? Or: what does it really mean to be free?

The Historical Background

In order to do justice to a discussion of the contemporary theatre scene, some historical contextualization is necessary. For Bulgarian theatre is a young art form. In fact, the first Bulgarian plays were not, strictly speaking, Bulgarian: they were a Serbian comedy and a German melodrama, both produced in Bulgaria in 1856 – a cross-cultural influence thus having informed even the first 'Bulgarian' theatre productions.

The first Bulgarian theatre group as such was founded by Dobri Voinikov in 1865. Significantly, the company was based in Braila, Romania, outside Bulgarian national territory. This was in order to avoid the censorship imposed by Turkish traditions and the influence of the Greek Orthodox Church within the country – a censorship of themes such as independence and the nation's cultural revival. It was only in the twentieth century, in 1907, that a fruitful collaboration between two Bulgarian companies – 'Foundation' and 'Tears and Laughter' – at last led to the formation of the first Bulgarian National Theatre, which, once established, soon became the focus of theatrical life within the country.

During the second decade of this century, dramatic literature became dissociated from other forms of literature and related arts, since most theatre of the period was based on adaptations and translations rather than on Bulgarian playwriting. This first phase of Bulgarian theatre was characterized by the dominance of a 'bourgeois' theatre, complete with the traditional *mise en scene* of European texts, focused around the work of a few well-known authors – Ibsen, Chekhov, Strindberg, Hauptmann, and others.

At the end of the Second World War and the beginning of the Communist era, this bourgeois theatre was replaced by one focusing on issues such as class struggle and revolution. While many texts were imported from Western Europe, the censorship of certain themes and forms meant that only those plays which criticized capitalism or painted the horrors of the American Dream were deemed acceptable for staging, though the so-called 'classics' were generally permitted, as long as they did not obstruct party lines. Comedy was frowned upon because it was seen to be 'frivolous', and not to present anything 'constructive'.

Only very recently has Bulgarian theatre begun to emerge from the cultural isolation which had previously distanced it from the influence of the West and the avant garde. In the words of journalist and theatre historian Bouryana Zaharieva, 'the principal objective of Bulgarian theatre is therefore today to make up for lost time'. Zaharieva spoke at length about the difficult balance between exploring western techniques and theatrical developments, while yet trying to maintain and enrich one's own national identity. The Bulgarian theatre, she told us, is composed of a rich mixture of styles and forms, only recently influenced by western culture, and only recently able to produce – and allow to be heard – the voices of a younger generation of artists.

The Voice of Vaskresia Vicharova

Among the most interesting voices of the new generation is that of Vaskresia Vicharova (born 1957), who shocked the Bulgarian theatrical scene with her production of *Dzung* – roughly translated as *Ding Dong* – in 1987-89. Also performed in Urbino, Italy, in 1990, *Dzung* resulted from an adaptation of a text by the Russian author, Eugeni Charitonov. The show was unlike anything Bulgarian audiences had previously seen, and was welcomed by critics as 'the first postmodern production in Bulgaria'.

Dzung purports to tell a story from the beginning to the end, and then again from the end to the beginning. Lacking any 'plot' in the classic sense, it starts before the arrival of the audience and ends after they have left the playing space. Vicharova, who believes that it is particularly important to work in non-traditional theatrical venues, has also performed this piece in the streets and squares of Sofia – the first instance of street theatre in Bulgaria.

Dzung is characterized by its very strong emphasis on the visual. Most importantly, the piece depicts a number of actors whose physical movements are impeded by a range of mechanical objects attached to their bodies. These structures were designed by architect Zarco Uzunov, a close collaborator of Vicharova's, whose work is carefully integrated into the performances: for instance, a mask covers half of the face of an actor, thereby limiting his use of the face to convey meaning through facial expression, with the result that the other half of the face must somehow make up for the half which has been covered.

Similarly, when a metallic apparatus is attached to the arm of an actor, it limits his ability to move his arm in certain directions. The actor must, therefore, find movements which convey meaning in alternative ways. In another exercise (videoed in a teaching workshop format), a female silhouette is visible, though trapped in a plastic bag or body sack: every time the body contracts, the performer emanates a sound, as though the shape of her body were speaking. Otherwise, the performance is silent.

This kind of physical experimentation – with gesture and body language as well as with mime – was shocking to an audience more accustomed to naturalistic and realistic adaptations of texts by Western European authors. But although Vicharova's work is highly experimental and original, particularly within the Bulgarian context, there is a sense in which her style is also distinctively Bulgarian. For instance, her work involves a complex weaving together of folk tale and myth with contemporary street language and the specialized vocabularies of the educated elite – all combined into a fragmented language used by characters who tend to speak at, rather than with, each other.

Vicharova's use of overlapping and fragmented dialogue is reminiscent of Caryl Churchill's. It recalls, for instance, *The Lives of the Great Poisoners*, a performance piece which involves dance and song as well as physical and text-based theatre, and which conveys the idea that the characters might as well be speaking different languages. In Vicharova's use of fragmented language in *Dzung*, however, the effects of the years of censorship are manifest: in this she seems to be in step with (or perhaps leading the way for) some of her contemporaries. Certainly, a notable lack of interaction between characters is strangely characteristic of contemporary Bulgarian theatre.

The Rare Beauty of 'Playing Beyond'

Vicharova's most recent production, *Playing Beyond*, exemplifies this modern Bulgarian approach to theatre. We were fortunate enough to see this in its first and only full production, in October 1991 – a performance 'staged' at night in an abandoned cave in the suburbs of Sofia, with lights rigged in the trees and along the jagged rock of the cave walls. With most of the audience, we were driven by bus out to the deserted cave: an abandoned archeological mine in the hills outside Sofia. On the way the bus ran out of petrol, and we had to wait for an hour while passing cars were stopped and petrol was siphoned for us. The performance did not commence until we had arrived: we were, the company told us, the only western journalists who would ever see the piece.

In fact, *Playing Beyond* was performed for that one night only: it was more of an 'event' than a 'play', and the live video recording made during the performance added to its fleeting, temporal sense even as it created a lasting visual record. Performed by a group of very young student actors who study with Vicharova, the piece communicated to the audience in different languages and regional dialects, using jargons of different professions and areas of cultural concern. It alternated folk dancing and religious prayer with political and existential pronouncements about the present-day isolation of Bulgaria as a nation.

Extraordinarily evocative, *Playing Beyond* was an event of tremendous beauty. Despite the bitter cold, the young performers, notably Vesselin Dimitrov Mezekliev and George Toshev, gave all their energies and talent to a performance which was very much an ensemble piece held together by the spirit of the actors and the attention of the audience – occasionally distracted though they were by the fear that those climbing the cave walls would fall, or by the flashing light of the video camera.

Beyond this, though, the performance was held together by the will of the director: Vicharova stood at the rear of the cave gesticulating wildly throughout, as if conducting the 'music' of the actors' silence and sound. Thus this performance piece, which was created with no funding, no sets, and no text, became a postmodern spectacle unequalled in contemporary British theatres. It was more than spectacle, however: it also seemed to encapsulate the spirit of this moment in Bulgarian history, and to bring that moment into sync with the past through the use of quotation from folklore, prayer, and mythological sources.

In its final sequence, *Playing Beyond* offered an unforgettable image: a huge white dropcloth had been hanging along the opening to the cave throughout the performance, creating a fourth wall of sorts by separating spectators and actors from the hills beyond. This immense cloth was suddenly released from its bindings, and made a sudden thunderous sound as it fell and landed on the earth – a sound which emphasized the silence of both the actors and of the countryside. And, of course, the curtain which had separated the cave and the encircling audience from the hills was now gone: the fourth wall had quite literally been removed.

At this moment, Vesselin Dimitrov Mezekliev, the lead male actor who had crept under the curtain and out of sight a few minutes earlier, became visible: nude in the chill of the winter night, he danced away from the cave, curving his body in animalistic contortions which were at once beautiful and eerie. As he moved away from the lights of the cave, he became the centre of attention against the much larger backdrop of the hills beyond, dramatically lit. The world was, in effect, his stage, as he clutched at a Bulgarian version of the bagpipe and played the instrument loudly, seeming to become a version of Pan.

Playing Beyond, directed by Vaskresia Vicharova. Top: Vesselin Dimitrov Mezekliev, just before the huge drop cloth falls. Bottom: the rockscape setting, with actor George Toshev (centre).

As he slowly disappeared into the hills, as if engulfed by the encircling forest, the rest of the actors followed, seeming to blend with the hills and to 'become nature' as they moved further away from the audience in the cave. The performance ended with the sound of music echoing from the hills; the performers barely visible in the distance, the landscape the centre of attention.

Playing Beyond might not have been created in another context: not in any other cave or playing space, let alone any other country. Of course, comparisons can be made with the work of Peter Brook, or with groups such as the Living Theatre and Shared Experience: but Vicharova's work can be seen as distinctly 'Bulgarian', even as it challenges the norms of the accepted theatrical tradition of the country. Though Vicharova does tap into some elements of western avant-garde theatre, she uses the musical, gestural, and visual inheritance of her own country, therefore representing a progressive and alternative voice which not only counters the Americanization of the Bulgarian theatre and cinema, but which may also reach out to affect the theatres of the West.

Thus, she is currently preparing a version of *Faust*: which offers many possible interpretations in the contemporary Bulgarian context. Vicharova's *Faust* will be performed in a variety of languages, but will rely in its interpretation on Bulgarian myth and folklore as well as on the facts of contemporary economic and political life in the country. In this dramatic moment of political fragmentation, following the dismantling of the former Soviet Union, it seems somehow appropriate that Vicharova's work – which communicates through a transcultural and 'universal' form of language – should gain greater recognition in the West.

The Theatre Texts of Stefan Moskov

Among the other 'new theatre voices' emerging from Bulgaria, Stefan Moskov – born in 1960, and, like Vicharova, a graduate of the National Academy of Bulgaria – also stands out. With ten other graduates, he founded the first entirely private theatre company in Bulgaria – a company which, ironically, does not have a name. His reasons for founding it were related to what he perceived as the stifling atmosphere in text-based traditional theatres, where, he told us, with only rare exceptions 'performances are like walking books'.

Like Vicharova, Stefan Moskov therefore decided to privilege visual and musical elements, choosing to work collectively with his company in devising original 'texts' during the process of rehearsal. There are no technicians in the company, and everything is done collectively, from rigging the lights (if there are lights) to writing the script (when there is a script) to performing the plays – a collective working method not unusual in western theatres, but previously almost unknown in Bulgaria.

As Moskov told us: 'Before the revolution, technicians were members of the secret service who reported to the government about every breaking of censorship.' He was exaggerating, but partly serious: for Moskov, working collectively was a way of ensuring not only the quality of the work, but also the security of the company.

We saw a curious production of *Romeo and Juliet*, produced by Moskov's company and videoed for reference purposes. The piece is only loosely based on Shakespeare's original, and involved only a few 'living characters' (that is, characters played by living actors): Romeo, Juliet, Mercutio, the Nurse, Lorenzo, and the servants. The rest of the 'characters' are represented by statues. In Moskov's words, the performance is: 'interpreted as a tragedy, sung as a Bulgarian folk song, performed with statues, and represented before a group of tourists as if it were a musical'. The piece experiments with a number of theatrical genres, creating a piece of theatre which offers considerable scope for audience interpretation and imagination.

Despite one or two common directorial strategies, Moskov's style is very different from Vicharova's. In Moskov's work, a mood of dark comedy prevails – a mood which is self-conscious, seeming to evaluate

Top: a scene from the production by Borislav Tchakrinov for the Off-the-Canal Theatre of David Mamet's *Sexual Perversity in Chicago*. Bottom: from Peter Pasov's production of *Don Quixote* with the InterMa puppet theatre (photo: Silva Buchvarova).

toward unexplored frontiers, or use non-theatre spaces, etc. I produce many foreign texts, simply because the Bulgarian texts seem old-fashioned. Most young people today prefer to go to discos, or to the cinema. This is why I have tried to create a certain atmosphere in our theatre. We organize jazz concerts, exhibitions, poetry and theatre readings, a school for directors, and we also show films, but not commercial films, because everyone else shows them.

Roussi Tchanev, a member of the company and a well known theatre and film actor, explained that 'while in the past theatre had a very official function, the Teatur zad Kanala simply aims to offer recreation and entertainment'. And he added: 'the majority of actors in the company are already famous through television, radio, or theatre, so the audience enjoys meeting them in the theatre bar. For young people this is very exciting. There is no distance between us and the audience, and this is still very unusual in Bulgaria.'

When, rather cynically, we hinted that perhaps after every revolution public figures suddenly become more visible – in fact, the previous day we had seen the Bulgarian Prime Minister himself on the street near our hotel – Borislav Tchakrinov replied: 'We have to watch these things, also Fidel Castro walks on the streets of Cuba without bodyguards.' The audience-stage relationship clearly has political implications in a country whose drama often takes place in 'real life'.

Voyeurism in Mamet – and Schnitzler

Though *Sexual Perversity in Chicago* is hardly a 'new' play by western standards, it is new to Bulgarian audiences. Tchakrinov would have liked to have staged it some time ago, but was not free to suggest (much less depict) its sexuality during the years of the Communist dictatorship. The set for Tchakrinov's production was very 'modern', and coloured almost entirely in bright shades of red, white, and blue – a reference to the national colour schemes of the USA and also of Pepsi Cola (a 'product' which in a remarkably westernized marketing strategy,

was distributed to the audience at the entrance to the theatre).

An element added by the director which we found particularly interesting was the representation on stage of a number of technicians who in the first act walk up and down the set while cleaning it meticulously, changing the scenery, or simply reading the newspaper. One of these technicians, in an obvious allusion to the censorship of the past, even records the performance onto video.

Tchakrinov tried to produce a similar effect in his earlier production of Anatol Schnitzler's *La Ronde* (1990). The video record of that production reveals that every time the protagonists tried to have sex, they were observed by bored military police. By way of contrast, in the second act of Tchakrinov's production of Mamet's play the voyeurs are not police, but technicians who seem to act as stage managers, hurrying on the action of the play, as if in the larger effort to help Bulgarian theatre to 'catch up' with the West.

In Tchakrinov's view of the play, this sense of cultural relativism is evident, but so is a more philosophical and introspective notion: 'In real life it often happens that one thinks one is doing something and ends up doing something completely different. So whereas normally actors require silence, here they are surrounded by a group of invasive technicians. In real life there is always someone trying to interfere with our lives.' The self-censorship which Tchakrinov effectively imposes within his production is thus framed by a clear recognition of the position of Bulgarian theatre, reaching toward an uncertain future, but always informed by the past.

Tchakrinov is also sceptical about the future of the nation. In his view:

It is frightening to think about what will happen here, especially about the fact that in trying to get up to date with Western Europe we may lose our identity. Our future is in the hands of the young, since the older generations can only try to survive. The main problem is that not much has changed in the cultural scene of Bulgaria, apart from the fact that we are all much poorer now.

This rather pessimistic view was echoed by one of the senior political figures with responsibility for the arts in Bulgaria: Nicola Vandov. Vandov is editor of the only theatre journal in Bulgaria, *Teatro*, and is the man responsible for theatre in the Ministry of Culture. Vandov's remarks revealingly set all the other interviews and discussion into a new framework:

In order to understand the range of changes, we have to know what was really the situation in the period of Communist dictatorship, when the government provided for all that was necessary for the existence of theatre, from subsidies to venues and personnel. Everyone who worked in the theatre had sufficient funds to do what they wanted. It is now very difficult for professionals in the theatre to understand that they have to learn to cope by themselves, because the freedom that we recently obtained will not solve economic problems.

In the last three years the Ministry has tried to offer some solutions, especially in 1991 – for example defending the right to autonomy of the theatres, so that nowadays it is the theatre practitioners who decide what to produce and how to produce it. The audience is therefore the only judge of production values – this is no longer the province of 'officials'.

This is obviously not new in the West, but for us it is a very unusual situation. Unfortunately, though, the need to fight in order to practice one's own profession the following year, the following month even, leads to the fact that many artists oppose the changes, and the Ministry of Culture now has a very bad reputation. But we have to remember that although what we're doing now will have a negative influence on the monopoly exerted by theatrical institutions, it will surely be a breath of fresh air for the arts. We will shortly start to subsidize different types of theatre, and this is very unusual for us because we used to subsidize only professional theatre. We would now like the town halls, foundations, and private enterprises to begin to sponsor theatre as well.

We are also trying to create a new structural unit within the Ministry of Culture, to be called the National Centre for the Theatre. Among its other responsibilities, it will determine the appointment of new artistic directors for the various theatres in the country. Naturally, this is only true for the five theatres subsidized by the state, while the civic authorities will decide about the seven theatres which they subsidize. Groups such as Vicharova's will unfortunately have a very rough time, even though the National Centre for the Theatre will have the right (and

the Ministry previously didn't have the right) to devolve funds to experimental theatre.

Vandov's words were both reassuring and disillusioning – reassuring in their implication that funds might finally be provided for experimental work such as Vicharova's, but disillusioning in their assumption of the possibility of determining a set of criteria by which such work could be assessed. To us, the phrase 'standards of excellence' came ominously to mind. . . .

'Godot' as Star Vehicle

After the interview with Vandov, we found ourselves wondering whether such inconsistencies could be resolved. We had been invited to a rehearsal of a new production by the Teatur na Narodnata Armia, or the Theatre of the People's Army – the name of which speaks for itself. Walking along the incredibly long and Kafkaesque corridors of the theatre building, the less public parts of which were in a sad state of disrepair, we certainly didn't get the impression that things were noticeably improving. And our ambivalent impression was reinforced when we met with the theatre's Administrative Director, Dimitri Todorov, who told us:

While previously we could organize up to fifty rehearsals for each show, we can now only have twenty five. This is the first time that theatre people have had to think about funds. Government subsidies hardly cover the wages and the administrative expenses, and they certainly don't take account of inflation. If we don't find sponsors soon, we'll be forced to close. The problem is that finding sponsors here in Bulgaria is not easy, because the nouveau riche are often dishonest since their wealth derives from the black market. Also, it is difficult to explain to a costume designer that he or she will now have to recycle old costumes, or to a set designer that there may not be sufficient funds to build a new set for the next production. And it is difficult to explain to the audience that tickets will no longer cost twenty five p [*sic*].

At the Teatur na Narodnata Armia, we not only saw some rehearsals and interviewed key directors and administrators, but were also given a guided tour from one of the country's leading actors: Josif Surtchad-shiev, whom we will always remember for his extreme kindness and touching insights. Our interpreter, language student Mariana Tosheva, impressed by Surtchadshiev's generosity, told us that he is, in Bulgaria, most directly comparable in status to Sir John Gielgud in England.

When Surtchadshiev later went out of his way to deliver production photos by hand to the concierge at our hotel, our interpreter explained that even though Surtchadshiev is extremely famous, his kindness was not entirely surprising. Just as the younger actors in Vicharova's company needed to gain recognition outside Bulgaria if their careers were to develop, so even a 'star' such as Surtchadshiev would clearly benefit from such western attention. We were rather surprised to learn that we were the first to record interviews and collect information from the Teatur na Narodnata Armia for some years.

We saw Surtchadshiev perform in an exhilarating and original production of *Waiting for Godot*. The audiences were on average quite young, and the show impressed us with its physicality and attention to detail in movement and expression. The middle-European character of the production was probably influenced by the director's Brechtian interpretation of the text, as well as by the skilled improvisation of the actors.

Josif Surtchadshiev played Vladimir, and somehow made the part come to life in a way which no English or American actor in our experience has done in recent years, as a man abandoned without a map in a post-revolutionary world. Interestingly, the production, which has been running in repertoire for over six years, is as successful and popular now as it was in the years of censorship.

Improvisation under the Dictatorship

We asked Surtchadshiev to tell us something about the importance of improvisation during the period of the Communist dictatorship. He replied:

Improvisation was a very important weapon during the years of dictatorship, when Bulgarians, like actors in other Eastern European countries, became accustomed to speaking with much mimicry and punning.

The theatre in which I work is the Theatre of the People's Army, and paradoxically censorship had little power for us. In 1980, we performed a Russian text which took place during the Second World War: it included a scene in which the protagonist was making love with a Polish girl in a concentration camp. Fifteen minutes before the curtain on opening night, the censors arrived – and no one knows who they were since officially there was no censorship in Bulgaria – and they informed us that we couldn't perform the scene as it was, because a Russian soldier would never have made love publicly.

There was a big crisis, because it was a very important scene, and couldn't just be cut. At the end, the director managed to work out a compromise by covering the two lovers with a big sheet. Naturally, one could see the movement underneath the sheet, and it was possible to hear the sound effects. The effect of the scene was intensified.

The image of the actors moving beneath the sheet recalled to our minds the image of Vicharova's woman in a body sack, creating sound only through the movement of her body and suggesting interpretations without words. Again, that which could not be represented had been intensified in performance by covering it over. A veiled form of freedom of expression, we wondered?

We put this idea to Leon Daniel, the director of *Waiting for Godot* for the Teatur na Narodnata Armia – a film and theatre director whom several people had referred to as the man whose 'style became history', and who was the first to stage Beckett and Brecht in Bulgaria. Daniel told us that:

During the first performances of my production of *Waiting for Godot*, six years ago, people were bored and often left the theatre. Only subsequently did audiences start to identify with the 'theatre of the absurd'. The same happened with Brecht's *Herr Puntilla and his Man Matti*, and now both shows are extremely popular. In Bulgaria, it is everyday life that is absurd. This is an example of how theatre influenced the ways in which people saw their own lives.

Daniel also commented on the economic

From Leon Daniel's production of *Waiting for Godot* for the Theatre of the People's Army, Sofia. Third from left is Josef Surtchadshiev, playing Vladimir. Photo: Ivan Iantchev.

circumstances affecting the development of theatre in Bulgaria:

Censorship curiously helped the theatre scene in that it forced actors and directors to think of indirect and metaphorical ways of expressing what they wanted, or to convey a certain political message. This is why the visual aspect became so important. One cannot express everything with words. Furthermore, the true strength of theatre during the Communist period consisted in the fact that it was the only means of contact with the other countries of Eastern Europe. In the last ten years, there has been a big intellectual crisis and now the question is whether it is possible to proceed or not. It's a question of survival.

A Bulgarian Miracle?

Daniels's next production will be of a play by the well known Bulgarian author Ivan Radoev. Called *Miracle*, and written in 1985, it belongs to the school of 'theatre of the absurd', though Daniel sees the play as influenced by a particularly 'Bulgarian sense of the absurd'. In his words, the characters are influenced by a particularly 'Bulgarian sense of the absurd'. In his words, the characters are

Bulgarian, Turkish, and Jewish people, and a Russian woman from the White Army. They are all very old, and represent a real cultural mixture. The text had been banned because of the Turkish character, who wasn't considered acceptable. All these people are very old, and belong to different cultural backgrounds, and this causes various arguments in the course of the play, although they discover in the end that they cannot live without each other, and like Didi and Gogo in *Godot*, they decide to stay together. This is the 'miracle' to which the title refers, and I hope this will be a message for the twentieth century.

The play raises a thorny issue for Bulgarian theatre and society: the representation – or

Poster for Caryl Churchill's *Top Girls* outside the National Theatre in Sofia.

Revolution, as history has repeatedly taught, is not enough, just as democracy is not enough to guarantee that any kind of 'freedom' will be constantly applied and respected. Whose freedom? Which freedom? Freedom from what, and for what? These are the questions which contemporary Bulgarian society, and consequently its theatres, will no doubt need to address in the months and years ahead.

As we travelled by taxi to the airport for our return flight, the driver's radio blared out what our interpreter told us was the news. To our ears, most of the broadcast was unintelligible. But suddenly two words were clear: Caryl Churchill. Churchill's *Top Girls* – a play which depicts the limitations of a capitalist mentality on the lives of contemporary working women, and which was one of the first plays to use the technique of overlapping dialogue in its representation of women from different centuries, from myth and history, gathered 'round a dining table to share their thoughts about their roles and the ways in which history has misrepresented them – was about to open at the Bulgarian National Theatre.

The irony of the situation was not lost on us. What will be conveyed in the translation of ideas, we wondered: which freedom will audiences find in this play, whose values will it seem to reflect, and for whose benefit?

marginalization – of Turkish people. Bulgaria is, at present, home to over a million and a half Turkish people – a considerable figure given that the total population is only around nine million. Yet there are, according to those we interviewed and the written sources to which we had access, no known Turkish theatres in Bulgaria.

We wonder whether the 'miracle' hoped for in the 'new' Bulgarian society might not be extended to include some representation of the Turkish peoples – whether, on the growing list of priorities and achievements of the newly 'free' society and in the theatre, there shouldn't also be a dialogue, a respect, and a legal recognition of the rights of the so-called minorities in Bulgaria, as elsewhere.

Acknowledgements

All quotations in this article are taken with permission from the transcripts of taped interviews conducted in Bulgaria in October 1991. Funds for the trip to Bulgaria were provided by Trinity Hall, Cambridge, for Gabriella Giannachi, and by the Open University's Academic Research Fund for Lizbeth Goodman. We would also like to thank Vaskresia Vicharova, who invited us to Sofia and organized most of the interviews for us, and Mariana Tosheva for her indispensable work as our interpreter. Without their good will and assistance, as well as the co-operation and hospitality of all those interviewed, it would not have been possible to research and write this article. A version of this article has also appeared in Italian in *Linea d'Ombra*, Milan, June 1992.

Update from Eastern Europe

Kate Raper
from Poland

Stary Theatre: Ensemble in a New Climate

ARTISTICALLY, Stary Theatre, Krakow, has maintained an impressive record since the 1950s. It has been a source of innovative directors including such giants as Swinarski, Jarocki, and Wajda, as well as a talented younger generation – Bradecki, Gzegorzewski, and Lupa. It has also been a focus for good actors and designers: quite simply, it is a company for which almost everybody wants to work.

Taking over the leadership of the theatre in September 1990, Tadeusz Bradecki was aware that the days of the big state companies in Poland were numbered. Such a luxury simply could not be sustained in the new economic climate. Despite the 'national' status recently afforded Stary and its legendary position, it was dramatically closed for several days in the autumn of 1991 before its promised subsidy was finally forthcoming.

Such stringent measures, followed by a parliamentary debate upon the fate of key theatres in the country, were necessary to ensure continued financial support from the Ministry of Culture. Currently this funding from the state still makes up eighty per cent of Stary's annual budget, although this figure is likely to be reduced in the light of Poland's dire economic situation.

What is interesting is how the theatre has responded to its new and unstable conditions of existence. In this respect Bradecki and Stary – the two are indivisible in the sense that he is democratically elected from within what he calls 'the republic' of the company – have avoided the easiest option, of at least partly commercializing their activities. This would have involved seeking private sponsorship, transferring all the 230 staff onto short-term contracts, and popularizing the repertoire. Although there have inevitably been some adjustments, and permanent employment has dropped from some 100 actors to 65, a brave decision was made to try to preserve the ensemble at all costs.

This ensemble consists of more than just the group of artists at its core: it also incorporates a set of working conditions and a shared product. In the case of Stary, these two criteria are inextricably linked. Rehearsal periods are as long as required, ranging between two and seven months, and if a production is not ready the opening date is put back.

This is not to say that publicity has no meaning, but rather that it is kept in perspective: artistic integrity is seen as more important. In spite of this, Stary has over 700 performances on its four stages every year. With fewer actors and the need to fight for its survival, it still produced a record twelve new shows last season to add to its repertoire of approximately 37 plays: this compares with an average output of four or five plays in previous years.

The choice of material and those chosen to produce it has also remained free from the constraints usually associated with times of insecurity. Despite criticism, Bradecki began his tenureship by launching a season of classic Polish drama – intended both to reaffirm the spirit of Stary and to address the burning questions concerning Polish identity which have emerged from all the political changes.

The plays included Slowacki's *Fantazy*, which he directed himself, *Wesela*, by Wyspianski, produced by Wajda, and Gombrowicz's *Slub*, directed by Jarocki – a true piece of craftsmanship, with performances of absolute precision from the most experienced actors such as Radziwilowicz and Trela, as well as inexperienced ones like Kusmider, who has just graduated from PWST, the state theatre school in Krakow.

The production won the main prize in Warsaw, and was played this January to great acclaim in Paris at the Odeon Theatre. In addition Bradecki brought Jerzy Gzegorzewski back to Stary, the first time he had worked there since the late 'seventies, to create his own magical adaptation of Tolstoy's *The Death of Ivan Illych*, in which Jan Peszek played the lead role.

This may sound like a catalogue of reputable work from any national theatre of a certain standard. What is much more exciting is that work of this level is springing from a structure in flux, for the last eighteen months have seen the relevance of the stable ensemble and the whole model of the theatre actively questioned. Is the policy of keeping actors on life contracts essential, or does it make them complacent? Is the long rehearsal period simply an indulgence, or integral to the quality of the work? Will Stary become a relic of the former Arcadian age in the arts, or can it continue to be a focus for challenging, high quality theatre?

Having spent some time there – five months in 1989 and ten months in 1990-91, directing *The House of Bernarda Alba* – I would say that the decision to question rather than avoid the issue or blame circumstances was the right one. The conclusions that led to a policy of preservation, with certain important changes, were undoubtedly justified.

Preservation may seem a retrograde or conservative approach in the context of the 1980s and 1990s. In the case of Stary it has proved the opposite. The decision to stand by certain principles, conditions, and indeed artists has sprung from a genuine self-enquiry, which has created the realization that with a fresh understanding of its direction and role Stary can continue to flourish.

This is evident in many areas, some of which sustain previous trends – for instance, the policy of inviting foreign directors to work with actors from Stary. Thus, Robert Scanlon of the New York Repertory Theatre is this year producing Mamet's *Speed the Plough*. Bradecki has also perpetuated the tradition of encouraging young directors, and the theatre has begun to open its doors more regularly to the work of other com-

panies. Last year Roberta Carreri visited from Odin with *Judith* and *Traces in the Snow*, and Peter Brook with actors from CICT was proposing to work with the company in 1992.

In a completely new field Stary has begun to develop some practical links with smaller experimental groups. The world of theatre is more tightly knit in Poland, and divisions between larger companies and 'avant-garde' groups have never been as rigid as in Britain: thus, both Grotowski and Kantor worked at Stary before they set up independently, and recently there has been more active contact between Stary and Gardzienice, Staniewski's group from Lublin.

In addition Bradecki himself was invited by Richard Gough and the CPR in Cardiff to lead a workshop in their Director Training Programme. This took place last February, when he explored Büchner's *Woyzeck* with ten actors and directors – an experience which has strengthened his belief that, although Stary has not had in-house training in the past, specialized classes and workshops should be incorporated into the work pattern of the theatre in the future.

The stable company is difficult to justify in 1992. In Britain it has barely existed for ten years. In Poland, only around twelve of the seventy state-funded theatres are currently open. In the midst of this, Stary's survival is taking a very positive form, and work continues without economics being allowed to dominate. Lupa, who has just finished producing a performance based on Rilke's *Malte* which lasts twelve hours and is played over three evenings, is a good indication of this. His work, which is mystical and extraordinarily atmospheric, is loved by the critics, but plays to small houses. The rehearsals took seven months, and Stary is one of the only theatres where these conditions can still be accommodated and plays continue to be produced.

At the moment Gzegorzewski is starting another project, and Bradecki is writing the scenario for his next piece, based on a novella by Jan Potocki. The theatre is still largely full, and with seat prices comparable with those of the cinema, the audiences are refreshingly young. Even though contracts are no longer for life, new actors and directors are still being taken into the theatre from the state drama schools. The mechanism has not collapsed, sold out, or become fossilized: if anything it is more open, vital, and ready to face the challenges ahead.

Joe Cook
from Czechoslovakia

The Second Act is Called Crisis

AFTER STRUGGLING to survive over four decades of rigid government control, theatre in Czechoslovakia is struggling to survive freedom. Like every other sector of society, theatre is having to deal with the enormous problems of transition from life under a totalitarian system to the free-for-all rush of a liberal, market-based democracy.

Chronic financial difficulties, organizational havoc, and a tangled web of legislation have conspired to produce an atmosphere of uncertainty and apprehension over what the future will bring. All in the professional theatre communities of both the Czech and Slovak Republics agree that 1992 has been the toughest year since the 'velvet' revolution of 1989, the real danger being that many theatres, especially provincial ones, face collapse.

State subsidies have been held at their 1989-90 levels, which after accounting for inflation, has meant a drop of between 30 and 40 per cent in real terms. And this is compounded by the fact that, thanks to general economic hardship, a night at the theatre comes low on the list of priorities. For now that the media are at liberty to report and comment as they see fit, people have no need to read the subtext of the latest production for an inkling of the political truth. Audiences have declined by as much as 20 per cent in some cases, and ticket prices have had to increase, putting theatre

even further out of reach for a nation having to count every Koruna.

To counter such dramatic falls in revenue, theatre companies are trying every trick in the cost-cutting and fund-raising book. Actors are no longer on what amounted to state pensions for life. Most companies have trimmed their acting staff and introduced one-year and three-year contracts, with payments geared to productivity, and there is an increasing reliance on part-time and freelance artists. Companies are also trying to tour more often, since performances away from home can earn treble the usual box-office receipts. Management, publicity and public relations skills are being developed, and corporate sponsorship is being sought – with some success – from foreign firms.

Theatres are sub-letting parts of their premises, and there is a trend, particularly in the Czech Republic, to broaden the use of theatre buildings to incorporate other art forms. Czechoslovakia is discovering 'arts centres'. But for all the attempts at generating more income and the internal restructuring – since the 'velvet' revolution many company directors have been replaced and replaced again – there is only so much that theatre people can achieve through their own efforts

Thus, by far the greatest constraint on the theatre's future development is a lingering state bureaucracy rooted in the institutionalized mentality of the Communist era – which cannot or will not respond with either the agility or the speed that the situation demands. Professional theatre managers, fully aware of the economic climate and not greedy in their demands, are exasperated by what they see as the government's failure to release theatre from its administrative bond to the state.

Theatre in the Slovak Republic and the Czech Republic is financed and administered in separate and quite different ways. And although there are difficulties common to both professional theatre communities, the situation in Slovakia is better than in the Czech lands of Bohemia and Moravia.

While still strapped for cash (its 1992 budget is worth 30 per cent less than in

1991), the Slovak Ministry of Culture directly supports all 23 professional theatre companies, the National Theatre Centre,[1] and also *Javisko*,[2] which is the country's 67-year-old theatre journal. It has a closer working relationship with theatre than its Czech counterpart, and is much more responsive to its needs.

The Ministry is progressive in its funding of experimental and alternative theatre; administers the Pro-Slovakia Fund, from which groups can seek expenses for one-off projects; is drawing up legislation to protect its stock of theatre buildings from commercial intrusion and the threat of restitution (whereby the original owners of property confiscated by the state after the 1948 Communist takeover can reclaim their buildings and land); and is looking into ways of funding the theatre companies and transferring responsibility for the theatre buildings to the local authorities – 'sale and lease back' by any other name. But things are far from easy, and there are loud calls for a reduction in bureaucracy and a change of approach.

The Slovak National Theatre, based in Bratislava, employs some 900 people, and has two drama houses and the state opera house. Despite seeing its 1991 budget shrink in value due to inflation by 40 per cent from the previous year, it managed to break even, thanks mainly to the growing international reputation of its opera, which tours overseas and to festivals, and is visited at home by coachloads of Viennese opera-goers – thus attracting sponsorship from the giant Austrian Industries conglomerate.

As the National Theatre's director, Dusan Jamrich, says, 'We are lucky that opera has an international audience.' The National's drama, on the other hand, has seen its audiences drop by up to 20 per cent, and can only manage to generate between 10 and 15 per cent of the money it requires, the rest being dependent upon state subsidies.

Petr Mikulík, director of the National's dramatic ensemble, says that 1992 will be the last year of reasonable money for theatre. The National will be all right in the long run because it is a broad-based institution. But theatres in the countryside will face more of a problem, and some may well disappear. Maybe at the National we will have to include more commercial theatre in our repertoire in the future. But we won't differentiate between types of audience or types of theatre – whatever happens we have to maintain artistic standards.

Other Slovak companies face similar problems. William Hriedal, who is director of the Theatre of the Slovak National Uprising from Martin in central Slovakia – and one of the few Slovak company directors that remain from pre-1989 days – says that his company is facing a crisis due to many of his best actors leaving for Bratislava in search of more lucrative work. This, as one actor from another company pointed out, is hardly surprising when one considers that the 35 actors and directors among the company's 120 staff, are paid far less than the SNU's administrators.

Theatre Group Stoka, an experimental collective formed by director Blaho Uhlár and designer Milos Karasek, complain of slow decision-making by the Ministry of Culture having left them rehearsing and preparing shows without the money for props, equipment, and costumes. They have, however, found themselves rehearsal premises – in a disused warehouse symbolically situated between the former Ministry of Interior's police headquarters and the National's 'Mala Scena', or Small Stage.

Theatre Korzo 90, reformed after its enforced closure in 1971, and housed in a new building (its original home having been returned to its pre-Communist owner), runs a tight ship with a staff of 29. Manager Petr Turcík reports that the theatre has seen no decline in audiences, which he puts down to a new generation's interest in their work plus the return of the company's old audience prior to its closure. However, the company has had to cancel tours due to lack of money.

Formed at the beginning of 1991 out of the old Theatre Institute, the National Theatre Centre in Bratislava documents and records Slovakia's theatre culture. It runs a video library and a publishing programme, organizes festivals and exhibitions, and is moving more towards the promotion of

Slovak theatre abroad. Dana Sliuková, its deputy director, sees the Centre as important for two reasons: 'It's necessary to support theatres during the present climate, and the existence of the Centre helps to stabilize the position of theatre in Slovakia. And it can be used as a means of promotion abroad. It's vital for our theatre to make contacts abroad and to create a position whereby they can compare their work, critically and technically, with theatre from other countries.'

Whereas the former Theatre Institute had a staff of nearly 70, the NTC operates with a staff of 26. It is striving to create foreign links, but it cannot afford the computers it needs to make its work more efficient, and its building is under threat of restitution from the Franciscan monks who once had their monastery there. (The Communists, with due cynicism, installed a museum of atheism and a pub in the building, of which NTC occupies the upper floors.)

All Slovak theatre companies will get their 1992 allocations from the Ministry of Culture in quarterly payments – which begs the question: what if there is no money left in the kitty come the last quarter?

The Czech Ministry of Culture supports the National Theatre and the Theatre behind the Gate (2), both in Prague; the lobby group Divadelni Obec (Theatre Community);[3] the theatre journal, *Svet a Divadlo* (*The World and Theatre*);[4] and also the Theatre Institute in Prague.[5] Additionally, it has a small provision for one-off projects.

The capital's thirteen other professional companies and all the Czech provincial theatres are funded by the local authorities. And therein lies the rub, since the local authorities receive their money from the Ministry of Finance, ruled by Vaclav Klaus – and Mr. Klaus feels that culture is a luxury to be enjoyed when it can be afforded.

Local authorities, now free of central planning, administer their budgets according to local needs, and, naturally, health-care, education, social services, and civil works come first. However, because town councils have traditionally funded theatre, there is a reluctance to divert funds away from

culture. The result of this tension is that some local authorities attempt to load their support of theatre companies with tacit (and in some cases not so tacit) political pressures to alter artistic direction. In Bohemia there is no money for 'alternative' theatre.

Other local authorities continue to fund theatre at the expense of more pressing needs. Ondrej Hrab, one of the new generation of theatre directors, manages Projekt Archa, based at the premises of the now closed E. F. Burian Theatre in Prague, offered this astonishing example: 'I know of one town in the Northern Moravia where approximately 30 per cent of the town hall budget goes on theatre. In that town they have a big problem with asbestos pollution and they need a great deal of money to deal with it, but they still fund the theatre. Although I'm a theatre person, I would never do such a thing.'

Hrab is one theatre director who has a clear grasp of what needs to be done to ensure the future viability and survival of Czech theatre. And his ideas are radically different from the Czech tradition:

In Czechoslovakia the word, *divadlo* (theatre) means the building, the company, the art, the staff – everything. It's a catch-all phrase that's outlived its definition. People have to forget about the past and think about the future. For us, it is necessary to start by admitting that we don't know what theatre is, but we do know that we have to support theatre.

The main problem is that while things have changed, cultural institutions have remained the same. While our economy has a programme for transformation towards privatization, no programme has been developed for the transformation of the state arts policy.

Under the system of local authority funding, each company carries a complement of staff who deal with the money allocated – staff who are not wholly answerable either to theatre company or town council. Aside from any political implications, this bureaucratic link – a remnant of Communist planning and job creation – is causing theatre managers almost to tear their hair out in frustration: while actors have been fired and new drama graduates cannot find positions, there exists no legal framework to lay-off staff who, according to Hrab, are unproductive and who work 30 per cent for the company and 70 per cent for officialdom.

Obvious to everyone except the powers-that-be is the need to create something along the lines of Britain's Arts Council. Divadelni Obec campaigns for greater autonomy for theatre companies, and has undertaken its own research into how other countries finance their theatre. They've held talks with the French, Dutch, Belgians, and Germans, and in June looked at the American model of funding.

'We want a mix of state subsidy and self-finance', says Bohumil Nekolny, its General Secretary, 'and we want independent control of finance.' It is only this, he asserts, that will enable theatre to stand on its own feet and to shape its destiny. President Havel's personal adviser on cultural affairs, Petr Oslzly, a dramaturg with Brno's Theatre on a String, is under no illusions about what needs to be done: 'There is only one possibility', he says, 'and that is that there should be a state budget for an arts council independent of the Ministry of Culture.'

The Ministry of Culture lacks imagination in its approach to the problems facing Czech theatre. It can deal with day-to-day problems, but has no overall programme for theatre in the Czech Republic. In Slovakia they have good people at their Ministry. Our Minister, Milan Uhde, may be a good playwright, but he's not a good theatre manager, and his Ministry fails to understand that the system of funding in Czechoslovakia, via the town councils, is not the norm in the rest of Europe. It is very protective towards the National Theatre in Prague, but not towards the national theatre of the Czech Republic.

For its part, the Czech Ministry of Culture says that it is aware of the problems facing theatre companies, but admits that its hands are tied by the system of government funding. According to Zdenek Hess, a former actor seconded to the theatre department at the Ministry:

The ministry only funds the National Theatre and Behind the Gate: our contact with the rest of the theatre community is only indirect. The local authority system of funding gives rise to many conflicts of interest. Furthermore, town councils receive their money in quarterly payments, and by the end of the year they may run out of money. For theatres in big towns – Ostrava, Brno, Prague – the situation is more propitious, but regional theatres will have a struggle, to say the least.

The Czech National Theatre, with over 2000 employees, comprises the Smetana Opera House, the recently restored Theatre of the Estates, and the splendid theatre building overlooking the River Vlatava – the one from which Vaclav Havel and Civic Forum directed the 'velvet' revolution. But the National is on the road to privatization, and from 1 April 1992 all three buildings were split into independent operations with a separate management structure and a private company or foundation helping to run them.

The legendary Magic Lantern has already been privatized, and now makes a profit by serving up an undemanding repertoire of light entertainment and cabaret to Deutsch-mark wielding tourists. And once the National is split up and functioning in a pseudo-privatized manner, the Ministry will only have Behind the Gate to worry about.

Not that they'll have to worry about the Balustrade for too long. 'Behind the Gate is a special case within the Ministry', explained Mr. Hess. 'It was formed by Otomar Krejca in the 'sixties out of the National and suffered greatly during the Communist era. Our Minister, Uhde, is a close friend of Havel (who cut his theatrical teeth at Behind the Gate), and it is seen as a case of the state repaying a moral debt.'

However, the Ministry feels that this special relationship cannot last. 'For one thing there is an election this year (June 1992), which may result in a new minister who could review the arts policy.[6] It is also probable that Behind the Gate will be privatized. Otomar may propose his own project, which probably won't be too difficult due to his reputation, particularly abroad.'

Which is all right for Otomar and Behind the Gate. But for the rest of Czech theatre, and Slovak companies too, the struggle to keep the show on the road is taking its toll on morale. There is even talk of a loss of culture. 'We fear a loss of indigenous culture', remarked an official within the Czech Ministry of Culture. 'Somewhere along the line, countries like Belgium, Denmark, and Switzerland have lost much of their indigenous culture and they now tend to import their culture, their art. This is something we want to avoid.'

As Ivan Vyskocil, executive head of the actors' union, Herecka Asociace, struggling to represent around 2000 members with a full-time staff of two, pointed out, 'We can import all the industry, medicine, and products we need, but we cannot import Czech culture.'

Thanks to one timely piece of legislation – requiring all theatre buildings subject to a restitution claim to remain as theatres for at least ten years after reverting to their original owners – one important house and company in Prague has been spared the ultimate indignity: this is Theatre Labrinth, formerly the Realistic Theatre (where the very first meeting of stage people took place following the outbreak of the 'velvet' revolution), and which is home for the company of the same name, besides providing offices for the journal *Svet a Divadlo* and the lobby group Divadelni Obec.

When the building returned to its original, pre-1948 owner, he found a buyer for it: a German who wanted to introduce a German repertoire to the main stage and a cabaret and beer-hall in the basement studio, in order to profit from the ever-increasing number of German tourists and businessmen who flock to Prague. 'Can you imagine it', said company dramaturg Vlasta Gallerova, clearly horrified at the prospect, 'all that vulgar humour and beer drinking. It would be dreadful.' Quite. Unable to realize his plans, the potential buyer lost interest. But the building remains on the market, although the company are 'secure' for at least a decade.

It is cruelly ironic that after enduring four decades of isolation and artistic oppression, and having played a leading role in achieving a democratic Czechoslovakia, the theatre world now finds its livelihood and future in serious jeopardy. If theatre companies can survive until 1993, they may get additional revenue from a new tax system designed to encourage personal and corporate donations to culture. But whatever prospects lay over the horizon, Czechoslovak theatre has a huge fight on its hands. How it manages to get out of its (yet again) seemingly impossible situation remains to be seen.

In December 1990, the Czechoslovak playwright, more recently state President Vaclav Havel, said: 'The happiness is gone. The second act is called crisis. The crisis will be chronic and then the catastrophe will happen. Finally the catharsis will come, and after that everything will start to go well.'

Notes and References

1. National Theatre Centre. *Deputy Director:* Dana Sliuková. *Address:* Frantiskánská 2, 813 57, Bratislava, CSFR.

2. *Javisko. Editor:* Anton Kret. *Address:* Námestie SNP c12, 815 85, Bratislava, CSFR. *Published:* ten times per year, annual subscription £20 (includes abstracts in English and French).

3. Divadelni Obec. *General Secretary:* Bohumil Nekolny, c/o Divaldo Labyrint, Stefanikova 57, 150 43, Prague 5, CSFR.

4. *Svet a Divadlo. Editor:* Ondrej Cerny. *Address:* Stefanikova 57, 150 43, Prague 5, CSFR. *Published:* ten times per year, annual subscription £20 (includes abstracts in English).

5. Theatre Institute. *Foreign Department:* Mirka Potuckova, Celetna 17, Prague 1, CSFR.

6. In fact, Uhde remained Minister of Culture.

Ben Payne
from Russia

Trying to be Dead Playwrights

WHEN perestroika legitimized the social criticism for which the Russian theatre had been the only forum during the 'years of stagnation', playwrights such as Gelman, Galin and Petrushevskaya came to prominence. The breaking of the wave of so-called 'black' plays, however, also coincided with the beginning of the disintegration of the society which they scourged.

This process complete, who and what is to follow? One answer is that of the young dramaturg at the Oleg Tabakov Studio in Moscow: 'There is no generation of young playwrights. In fact, one could say there is no younger generation at all.'

If this proves to be an exaggeration, it is important to understand the emotion which prompts it. For one thing is certain: the collapse of the former Soviet state's attempt to define all aspects of its culture casts a long shadow. This presents unprecedented challenges to those who continue the tradition of Russian writing for the theatre.

Yelena Gremina and Mischa Ugarov are members of the Klub Novoi P'iesy (Club of New Playwriting). Gremina recently attended a conference of women playwrights where some participants said they had not written anything for two years. Was it a disease brought on by the chaotic circumstances in which they lived?

Gremina herself believes that this is exactly the reason why there has never been such an exciting time for new playwrights in Russia. A great diversity of themes is now open for exploration, and of these she believes the most important is money: 'This was also the great theme of the nineteenth century, of Dostoievsky and Ostrovsky. Soviet reality did not recognize it, so here is a line of tradition which can be rediscovered.'

The dislocation from tradition is a legacy of socialist realism which affects even language itself. Ugarov's play *Grammar According to Grot* examines the implications of the Bolshevik revision of the Russian language system, including the removal of 'unnecessary' letters of the alphabet. These go beyond mere linguistics for two adolescent schoolchildren (the boy possibly a young Lenin), who in the course of their studies are also trying to discover their sexuality.

The reception of the play's reading in St. Petersburg tended to focus on its debt to Freud, while Ugarov insisted that the debt to Marx was as large – a discrepancy which

can perhaps be traced to the fact that this is only the first generation to have been able to read the former, while the latter is, at the very least, unfashionable at the moment (more recent thought which reinterprets both, such as that of Lacan, has as yet only unevenly absorbed).

Ugarov's play is both an uncovering of the subconscious levels of reality and of the idea that language informs psychology, not the other way round. In this he seems to be at one with another colleague, Oleg Yuriev, since both subvert socialist realism and break with those playwrights who used the realist form to examine the society which perestroika was seeking to reform. Indeed, the whole process by which 'reality' is perceived is now open to question.

Three of Yuriev's plays, *A Little Pogrom in a Railway Station Snack Bar* (1984), *Comic Stories for a Theatre of Shadows* (1987), and *The Little Song of Little Songs* (1989), in varying ways confront the premise that history advances in straight lines. *A Little Pogrom* takes as its remote yet resonant starting point a Jewish family trapped in a railway station snack bar in 1902 by an advance guard of anti-semites while awaiting the express train to Vilnius. This train is actually carrying the main body of the lynch-mob to the town.

The central poetic metaphor is anchored in the dramatized version of the tale of the prophet Jonah (who was angered by the imperfect audience the citizens of Nineveh made for his prophecies) which the family perform to distract their waiting killers. Yet the snack bar is only an apparent starting point, for the play 'self-destructs' three times during its course. It is successively revealed (each time just as the pogrom is threatened to start) that what we are now watching is a rehearsal of a present-day amateur Jewish theatrical group; then a rehearsal of Russian actors in a future where no one has seen a Jew. At the point of final implosion, the dispersal of the Russian actors' rehearsal, the young Jewish boy of the original family suddenly returns with the scissors for which he was sent in the first scene. Finding himself alone, he begins to pray in Yiddish (whereas previously all the actors have spoken what would have been Yiddish or Hebrew as Russian). Thereby he is suddenly revealed as 'real', conjured out of the reductive system of illusion, and, as he prays, the sound of an approaching train is heard.

Yuriev's method is deliberately to collide history with fiction. Texts simultaneously form and dissolve in this revelation of history as, in his words, 'the horror of a mirror's errors'. The final image of a child seeking an extrinsic meaning from within a brutal, subjective world is itself a reflection of a contemporary reality which sees itself as bereft.

It would be ironic if the new cultural context actually marginalized such work more than in the Gorbachev era, but there are two potential dangers: the artistic polarization of the director and the playwright, and the changes the whole theatre industry will experience under a new economic system.

Ugarov, for one, is phlegmatic about any suggestion that the control of the 'means of production' could now be more open to the contemporary playwright: 'Directors will read a play of mine with interest, talk about it with pleasure – and then not stage it, perhaps for five years. Scripts have therefore to exist in time, they become more like literature. But, in any case, it's an illusion of directors that plays have to be performed.'

Here is a barrier of mutual mistrust. Playwrights perceiving that their work is 'literature', less and less a public form, can only serve to widen the gap between themselves and those directors who see theatre as the most public and immediate form of 'art'. Meanwhile, directors excluding playwrights from their creative processes further prevent the latter from developing a more spontaneous theatrical language. Current theatrical training seems not to enhance the bringing of the two together.

The recent premiere of a production at the Stanislavsky Memorial Theatre in Moscow illustrates this. Dani Ginkas comes from the 'directorial' family of Kama Ginkas and Genrietta Yanovskaya. Ginkas is training to be a director himself, and he wrote *The Bald Brunette* for his fellow trainee, Oleg Babitsky. A deliberate decision was made before rehearsals started: 'We have a saying on our director's course: "The best playwright is a dead playwright",' Ginkus says. 'Here the director is the author of the performance. So I gave Oleg the finished script and left him to rehearse it alone, without interference from me. I was trying to be a dead playwright.'

The Bald Brunette concerns two men who live in the same flat. The exact nature of their relationship is never made clear, and the play consists in the main of their circular games of language. Dialogue like:

THE BALD ONE: Why don't you leave?
THE BRUNETTE. I need this shit I live in. . . .

exhibits the presently prevalent absurdist influence – and it is in the absurdist genre that Babitsky has sought to place the production, most prominently in its set and sound design, which involved elaborate and expensive-looking costumes drawn simultaneously from the Renaissance and Paris kitsch, highly coloured expressionist scenery, and bursts of rock music by Mark Knopfler and the Russian rock star, Petr Mamonov.

Mamonov also takes the lead role of the Bald One. This, along with the design, may lead to the play being a popular hit: but, according to Ginkas, casting Mamonov caused complications in which parts of his speeches ended up being cut. The design, though he thought it 'beautiful', was 'really certain things in the aquarium to make the fish look better'. Ultimately he did not recognize his own play, which was actually about 'the sorrow, nostalgia, and isolation of two ordinary people'. The sacrifice of a text (whether by a living or dead playwright) to the idols of casting and presentation already shows perhaps more than a trace of western influence.

Yet the West can provide examples of good practice. Dmitri Lipskerov, whose *Underwear from Luxembourg* was given a rehearsed reading at London's Royal Court Theatre as part of last year's London International Festival of Theatre, was impressed by the approach such theatres have towards writers: in Britain, he recalled, 'they would ask me whether they could change a comma: here I'm lucky if I'm asked to attend rehearsals.'

However, Lipskerov's disinterest in politics was a cause of incompatibility with the Court, which, he believes, expected a play reflecting the current social upheavals in his country:

Our generation feels the weariness of all the others. Everything that happened before our birth is history, everything to come is eternity – neither are ours. The soul of a human being; two people meeting and the discovery of their relationship; love; hate; death – this is enough for a whole lifetime of plays.

His views are in accord with those of Mark Zakharov, the artistic director of the Lenkom Theatre, where Lipskerov's plays have been produced. When in London recently, Zakharov said that Russian theatre needed no longer to perform the oppositional political role of the past, but could return to the universal concerns which actually suited it best.

Zakharov also took a long hard look at the workings of the West End, since the coming of a capitalist system has obvious implications for the Russian theatre industry. However, he was impatient with doom-mongerers. The Lenkom, for instance, never received a substantial subsidy under the old regime, simply because it was often the last theatre to toe the party line.

Whilst commercial theatre may not be a reality yet in Russia, with spiralling inflation the new figure of the 'convertible' playwright earning foreign currency has already emerged. Lipskerov's own next project is thus a series of comic films for the BBC, written in collaboration with Grigori Gorin, introducing Russians to business practice. While Yuriev works on an academic grant in Frankfurt, for others commissions from German radio stations, for instance, are understandably attractive. This is a further source of division. Some critics are impatient with the legacy of 'poor theatre'.

If theatres like your Royal Court give their playwrights the right to fail, our new situation ought to give ours the right to succeed.

Gremina claims that it is not fear of failure that keeps her from writing for larger stages, but her own integrity. And she quotes Ostrovsky: 'Poverty is not a sin.' For her, sincerity is more important than money, and sincerity is more often found in intimate theatres with poor facilities – the poorer the better. She believes larger theatres – 'those with pillars' – are better suited to adaptations.

A production which manages to break this divisive mould is Nina Sadur's adaptation from a short story by Gogol, *Pannochka*, directed by Sergei Zhenovach at the Chelovek Studio in Moscow. This tiny venue on Skaterniy Pereulok was one of the many experimental 'room theatres' which suddenly appeared in the mid 'eighties – and one of the few which has survived to establish a formidable reputation.

The story – of a girl's death at the hands of a witch, and the subsequent temptation and destruction by her spirit of the philosopher-priest who prays for her soul – unites Sadur's own interest in the attractions and dangers of the unknown with her fascination for the figure of Gogol himself. For there is a strange biographical resonance in the writer's obsession with revealing the secret of the Slav soul which led to his own perdition under the influence of a religious obscurantist. If revelation is a central theme, it is also the guiding element of Sadur's dramatic technique:

I try to catch those tiny, fleeting points in a word or expression which render the whole world strange; when we see something new and mysterious. I was once sent from my Institute to a collective farm. The people I met there seemed to me to be from another planet or as if they had not yet been born. It was the feeling of shame at not having a language with which to communicate with them that led to my first play, *Strange Woman*.

It may be the simplicity of this approach which attracts directors like Zhenovach. It is certainly this which makes *Pannochka* so powerful. Sadur's work has also been produced by Kaminsky and Viktyuk. Building up a consistent relationship with one director is less important to her than the feeling that each has 'the same internal energy, the same sense of "play".'

Even so, though she would love to work collaboratively with actors and directors, she has also consistently been excluded from the rehearsal process. She has tried to establish her own company, but has had to shelve plans due to lack of money. Talk of a crisis in Russian theatre has become a cliché, but in the face of the uncertainty Sadur's attitude is necessarily modest 'I may not be able to change the theatre,' she says, 'but at least I can write.'

In Rita Much's recent interview in *New Theatre Quarterly*, Maria Arbatova indicated the lack of penetration that feminist discourses have had so far in Russian theatre. In *Pannochka*, for example, Sadur saw no reason to question the sexual stereotyping in the battle between Brut, the male philosopher, and the anarchic female succubus Pannochka. The theatre may have rediscovered sex after Communism, but not in a form which liberates any further: as Gremina puts it 'where once we had to write plays that included road-menders, now we have to include a naked woman.'

Sensationalism also has a darker side. In a recent festival of 'erotic' films, all the relevant scenes were in fact rapes. Feminism is often included in the wholesale rejection of the 'ideological' in art after socialist realism. Such avant-garde iconoclasm, exhilarating at first, often leaves a vacuum.

This can be seen in a 1989 play *Verona*, in which a couple engage in bedroom power games. Eventually the woman, tired out by the bickering, falls asleep. The man takes advantage of this by raping her. To arouse her, he tells her 'to think of something pleasant . . . something good and bright from your childhood.' The sense is of the grim relativity of all relationships.

At the point of orgasm, the man suddenly speaks the words of Christ in the Gospel according to St. John: 'Do not let your hearts be troubled. Exercise faith in God, exercise faith in me. In the house of my Father there are many rooms. Otherwise I would have told you because I am going my way to prepare a place for you. I am coming again and will receive you home to myself, that where I am you may also be. And where I am going, you know the way.'

Ironically, the couple are all too aware of their forsaken state. They have no faith in anything, least of all each other, and the blame for this is laid explicitly in the middle of their purposeless banter:

WOMAN: You sleep like a dead man. . . . You fold your arms on your chest, stretch out your legs. Completely identical.
MAN: That's because I was dead from the start. Is that clear?
WOMAN: Yes. The central idea of socialist realism.

The author of *Verona* is Alexei Shipenko. With a string of plays since the mid 'eighties, Shipenko has established himself as a sounding board of this generation which sees itself as lost. A former rock musician and acting student of Anatoly Vasiliev, Shipenko has had little difficulty finding theatres for his plays. It was Vasiliev who, in 1985, gave his first play, *The Observer*, to the young director Boris Yukhananov, who declared that its 'central point' was 'that one kind of music has ended and nobody knows what is to replace it'. *The Observer* focused on the crisis of the 'second', alternative, culture (of which Shipenko is both part and critic) represented by the enforced 'growing up' of Russian 'hippy' musicians with the advent of perestroika.

The theme of a Russian 'beat generation' without a beat is developed in later plays like *Verona* and *Archeology* (1988), whilst the title of *The Observer* can act as a useful tag for Shipenko's dramatic technique, since it reflects the oblique position he takes in relation to his characters. Often extraordinarily cruel to each other, their dialogue is rendered light and ironic, apparently, like Shipenko, feeling everything and nothing at the same time.

If this is a deliberately 'Shakespearean' approach, it is important to note that Shipenko is expressly writing 'only for and about himself'. In both *Verona* and *Archeology*, the central male character is a writer, a projection of Shipenko himself. In *Arche-*

ology, Lyosha, who is partly responsible, because of his apparently utterly detached attitude, for his wife's attempted suicide, is confronted by his friend, who believes that, as a writer, he ought 'to react in some way': 'What must I react to? To the world's sorrow? Or to the changes in society? I've got to. And I won't. I must but I won't. You know someone once said that the worst works of art come from the best intentions.'

And the friend is beaten up for his pains. Manifestations of evil and inhumanity are not so much conceived as problems of morality or politics but of form:

All my characters want to be better people – the best. They're trying to develop, but they have been born dead. Previously, the force of evil in Russian theatre had to be personified: this was also the case with socialist realism. Now, it is both the same and the opposite. Evil is *inside* the characters, but to reveal open direct conflict through character is a naive and silly way of writing plays. I transform it into something invisible. The conflict of these structures expresses more than this other obvious conflict. Character may not be more important than form.

The stream of images from a stock television adventure film or thriller, or Shakespeare's tale of 'star cross'd lovers' (*Verona*) are texts through which Shipenko creates his own dissonance. Each of the 'episodes' in *Archeology* is a meditation on the gravediggers' scene from *Hamlet*, and its form is like that of a prism.

An elderly geography teacher on the run from an asylum, her Second World War veteran son, the spiritually poisoned representatives of the present generation, 'the young people', and their equally disparate, rootless conversations, are all drawn gradually into perspective. It is Lyosha's much-abused wife who sounds the thematic resonance of the play's structure: 'All your life has been one long dream. Some endless, tasteless films or even episodes, separate parts. As if somewhere, the devil knows where, you looked over a whole mass of forbidden filth from a different life. . . . You've turned into an image on an acetate film.'

And sure enough, several episodes later, Lyosha watches crumbling footage of a journey to school in which everything has been erased except his walking feet: 'The feet which have taken me from one place to another, from that to a third, from year to year, step by step. And I don't see anything besides these feet. Nothing above them.'

Shipenko sustains the beat of the episodes, the frames, the steps of the journey from birth and innocence to confusion and death, with ruthless precision: a journey not of discovery but of loss. In the final episode, the endless game Lyosha used to play with his senile grandfather – in which the object is successively to name a town beginning with the last letter of a town previously named – is played by all the play's characters in a metro carriage, which becomes the focal point of the prism.

The search for redemption is depicted as a meaningless, already lost game (perhaps lost by a form of collective amnesia since the towns named do not even follow each other). Finally Lyosha is 'out' because he names a place which, his wife says, 'does not exist'. The truth is perceived as being only that which accords with what is real, yet this reality has been mercilessly revealed as entirely relative, entirely bereft.

Shipenko, who is sometimes referred to as an absurdist, insists that his plays are completely 'normal'. A middle-aged woman who saw *Archeology* in Kiev accused the whole company of being on drugs. Russian reality is currently far more disorientating. *Archeology* is not absurdist, but it is the end of a line of 'black' plays – a 'black' play in a darker shade of black, the last stage in the deconstruction of socialist realism.

NTQ Reports and Announcements

Peter Barnes

Working with Yukio Ninagawa

IT SEEMS that along with Bergman, Brook, Stein, and Strehler, Yukio Ninagawa is one of those theatrical directors whose every production becomes something of an event. His samurai *Macbeth*, *Medea*, and *The Tempest* were first seen at the Edinburgh Festival and were followed by the Japanese play *Suicide for Love* at the National, with its cast of 75 and its fifteen-minute snowstorm.

Ninagawa was born in 1935, became an actor working for the Seihai repertory company for twelve years and then, depressed at the plays he had to do, in 1968 formed his own Contemporary People's Theatre, performing small avant-garde dramas in cinemas late at night after the last film show.

In 1974 Tadao Nakane, a producer with the vast Japanese entertainment conglomerate, the Toho Company, asked Ninagawa to direct a series of classic plays. Since then they have worked on some twenty productions together, including *Hamlet*, *King Lear*, *A Streetcar Named Desire*, *Peer Gynt*, and *Oedipus Rex* with a chorus of 160, as well as a modern Japanese piece, *Tango at the End of Winter* by Shimigu Kumio. This play was performed at the 1991 Edinburgh Festival in English with an English cast prior to its transfer to London.

Ninagawa's directorial trademark is spectacularly choreographed stage effects – snowstorms, cherry blossoms, rivers, peacocks, and great chariots flying across the heavens. He says he is trying to break down the artificial barriers between different forms of theatre by combining ritual, naturalism, Kabuki, Noh, Hollywood musicals, and film westerns. It is not new. Some of us have been doing that, in our own way, for many years. But Ninagawa does it with some style, it must be confessed.

The following are some thoughts, purely personal, on the odd experience of working with this fascinating but politely evasive Japanese director. In trying to describe another human being, a writer should remember the Babylonian Talmud which has the first page missing. This means we have to begin at the second. So however much a man knows and learns, he must always understand he hasn't even got to page one.

Ninagawa is a very kind man, thin, slightly stooping, and unfailingly polite. So I cannot believe, for a moment, the story that he threw an ashtray at an actor – unless, of course, he threw it in Japanese. However, meetings with him take place in a cloud of unknowing. He has hit upon a method of walking backwards whilst greeting you with friendly gestures and warm smiles. Nodding happily and saying 'Hello, here I am', he gets further and further away, so that relationships, rich in good intentions, fade with him. The retreat, the unfulfilled promise of understanding, leaves a residue of sadness and frustration.

He surrounds himself with himself and looks like a man who has spent a sizeable portion of his life in flight, in rehearsal rooms or the theatre, believing real life is always happening somewhere else: like the horizon, it is just ahead of him somewhere.

Having mastered the art of silence like the Seer of Lublin, he talks little in rehearsals, preferring to illustrate points, if at all, physically. This is certainly a change, for the majority of English directors have been vaccinated with gramophone needles: their only defence against gnawing insecurity is the reassuring sound of their own voices.

Though he is not totally immune from coming out with the old, gnomic utterances, beloved of Peter Brook and other theatrical gurus – like telling an actress not to narrow her mind when she comes on stage – Ninagawa insists that actors work without a directorial voice incessantly nagging in their ears. Unfortunately some of them have been so brainwashed by years of exposure to the mind-numbing arrogance of a generation of native directors that they found the experience disturbing. On the other hand, those who normally took absolutely no notice of the director liked it all.

His directing method seems to be a traditional Japanese technique of instruction which is based on practice and continuous repetition. So from the first day the actors act out sections of the play in sequence, again and again. The learning process is Zen influenced, and long-winded instructions or explanations are almost totally absent. The teacher makes odd comments from time to time, but does not expect any questions from the pupil. If there are any, they are dealt with politely with a promise of full answers in the near future. These do not materialize. The teacher looks benignly on the efforts of the pupils, waiting patiently for growth, ripeness, fulfilment.

Through mechanical repetition the pupils are supposed to master the form so completely that they become capable of realizing any inspiration. The hand guiding the brush catches and executes whatever idea or picture surges into the pupil's mind, at the very moment the mind conceives it. In this method of gaining spiritual inspiration through repetition it is vital that both teacher and pupil have time, so there is no pressure for the teacher to harass or the pupil to be overtaxed.

Unfortunately, in the rehearsal situation, time is limited. Consequently there is constant pressure. The traditional method is distorted and has to be modified. But it remains very alien, for our western creative process is, to some extent, Socratic. Questions are asked, till hopefully – I was going to write, the truth is found, but that is impossible: questions are asked till hopefully solutions are found. Problems are man-made, solutions are there. It is difficult for us to leave our minds at home, though in the theatre it does tend to happen quite often.

More difficult is the language barrier. Courageously, Ninagawa was trying to direct an English cast whilst only speaking (and worse, only thinking) in Japanese.

Meanings come into being with language, so does mutual understanding. Without a common language we are alone, and (true horror) bereft of comedy. Explain 'My Grandmother died quite young so she never learned how to suck eggs', or 'I worship the ground her stockings drag on.'

Of course, with commendable Japanese efficiency, Ninagawa was provided with simultaneous translations at all times, but difficulties remained. 'I'm taking it all down in English. Is my translation accurate?' asked the interpreter. 'How should I know?' replied the Jewish survivor. 'My suffering was in Yiddish.'

Happiest when manipulating bodies in space, Ninagawa, like all internationally famous directors, has a great eye. This is essential, because only the eye leaps frontiers. Nowadays the image takes the place of the thing and the word: audiences see but do not listen, and the ear, the organ of the imagination, becomes redundant. Perhaps the present is too corrupt and the time for words is past. It has become too late.

Being so eye-oriented, it is surprising that Ninagawa is not a film director. He is surprised himself. He has made two movies, but feels they were not successful because he was inhibited by what he considered Tarkovsky's brilliance and the technical side of the medium.

He says with refreshing honesty that he became a stage director to overcome his social awkwardness: our lot did it to meet girls. He felt too self-conscious as an actor, and only as a director could he rid himself of his embarrassment at meeting new faces. Only in a rehearsal room could he feel free. Outside the rehearsal room it is indeed a great big world. I should know, I've tried to wallpaper it.

Seemingly open, he has suppressed his radical political beliefs, which did not survive the 'sixties. He has buried them just as he has buried his doubts about the validity of the theatre. They are too disturbing. There is a secret incentive in all of us as we grow older not to seek out conflicts in ourselves. If the machine still works, don't mess with it.

Ninagawa told me that two years ago he was very ill and thought he was going to die. Lying on his bed one night he saw a faint silver thread like a spider's thread, stretching up out from his body away into the darkness. I still believe this world hangs on nothing, but it is a beautiful image. Even revelations, it seems, come in beautiful stage pictures. . . .

I hear the sound of his footsteps but his voice doesn't reach me.

Deborah Middleton

State of the Art?

A report and commentary on *The Guardian* Panel Discussion on New Performance, held on 9 May 1992, with Kenneth Rea (theatre critic), Carolyn Graham (Manager of Event Planning, South Bank Centre), Lois Keidan (Performing Arts Officer, Arts Council), Richard Gough (Artistic Director, Centre for Performance Research), Denise Wong (Director, Black Mime Theatre), Anne Seagrave (performance artist), and Gavin Henderson (Artistic Director, Brighton Festival).

PART of the Brighton Festival was a weekend-long platform of 'innovative' performance accompanied by a *Guardian* panel discussion on New Performance. The works on show represented a wide range of performance styles, but try as it might the panel discussion found itself irresistibly drawn towards an equation of 'performance' with 'theatre' – indeed, a *mainstream* theatre which was not differentiated from its more experimental boundaries.

This definition of performance struck me as a startling anachronism, and one loaded with significance. Not all members of the panel were guilty – Anne Seagrave was present as a 'performance artist', and Lois Keidan's comments often brought the discussion back to both wider definitions and specific cases. Somehow, however, the relationship between theatre, performance, and performance art was never clarified, and therefore, the very subject of the discussion inadequately identified.

Perhaps it was a mistake to discuss such different genres (in content, form, and aim) in such close connection, and particularly dangerous to identify all aspects of performance with 'theatre', understood not as a generic title, but a particular form. Further, much performance work is in direct opposition to the mainstream with which it sometimes shares a name – and, as here, a discussion platform.

The *Guardian* discussion of 'theatre' alone lost sight of the range of forms embraced by the term 'performance', and of the many and various problems and qualities specific to those forms. This in itself must represent one of the major obstacles facing the artist for whom the theatre form is neither adequate nor appropriate.

Kenneth Rea, in the chair, opened the discussion by calling Britain the 'cultural weak link of Europe', and by asking how we can improve the cultural climate for both audiences and performers. Lois Keidan's excellent contribution to the discussion revolved around her plain assertion that there is no dearth of artistic work emerging in Britain, only a failure to nurture that work and to contextualize it. The problem is not a lack of quality, but the lack of a process through which to develop it.

There currently exists only one system through which performance *or* theatre can emerge – and that is the commercial one in which work often seems to be judged more by the quality of its publicity material than by its intrinsic quality. Gavin Henderson, as a promoter, confirmed that new work has great difficulty in surfacing and in coming to the attention of venues and promoters: artists are indeed at the mercy of their promotional material.

This is a system which is not only morally and socially unacceptable to a great many theatre workers, but it is also one which is fundamentally hostile to the development of the work itself. It was noted that in Britain there is a 'fundamental amateurism' towards performance work, in that performers are expected to invest – and lose – their own money in the lengthy and expensive business of establishing a reputation and attracting financial support. It was inferred that this had class implications.

Denise Wong made the important and connected point that there is not enough access to information and resources – no network to unite and guide workers and to provide a system whereby groups and individuals can assist one another.

In a discussion of the role of venues, Gavin Henderson pointed out the responsibility which the promoter has to the audience: it was necessary to establish a trusting relationship with the groups or individuals he promotes, and in this respect there is a general problem of access to the work of new companies.

There was general agreement among the panel that venues should take some responsibility for the nurturing of new work. Denise Wong suggested a system whereby a venue would encourage its own 'stable' of younger artists. A new Arts Council venture was also discussed which aims to give greater responsibility to venues for initiating and enabling new work. Gavin Henderson expressed his own wish that in future the 'showcase' itself should play a part in 'enabling' work as well as encouraging already established performances.

Funding, of course, was a major area of concern. A member of the audience expressed amazement and disgust at the 'absurd' social circumstances which funded artists are expected to endure, with no security from one project to the next. Anne Seagrave, as an unfunded artist, spoke of the drawbacks of continually counting costs, but asserted that being free of the time schedules which funding imposes is vital for her work. Gavin Henderson noted that in Europe performances are kept in repertory for years, whereas here the commercialism of the market economy pushes groups and individuals towards short-lived projects – and a consumer mentality, in which the emphasis on product far outweighs the importance of process. Further, the pressure to fulfil obligations to funding bodies and to recreate past patterns of success are drawbacks which funding inevitably brings in its wake.

There was a general concern that no alternative system to the commercial one had emerged which would be adequate to, and supportive of, the needs of performers and artists. Further, Richard Gough pointed out the central paradox of expecting work at once to create an alternative *and* to participate in the market: was it really possible to be experimental *and* to receive subsidy?

Experimental work must be granted the right to fail, to be unpopular, to take its own time and create its own rules – all of which was to question the very principles on which funding is generally given. And yet, in order to be able to create and experiment, the workers must be financially free, since not being dependent on the work providing an income allows risk-taking. Again this had class implications.

Given the commercial structure of the theatre-performance system, how can work be progressive and experimental? Gough pointed to the lack of work which 'causes a riot', has an effect. He pointed out that in order to exist at all we must try to be both acceptable and at the cutting edge. We want both good reviews and 'fire'. Where, he asked, is work that is 'difficult, resonant, shuddering'?

The creation of work which is experimental and challenging is not only desirable, but essential to the vitality and the relevance of performance. By their very nature, artistic conventions necessitate their own replacement.

A thing once spoken is already dead, reality lies somewhere beyond it and the thought has become petrified, so to speak. A manner of speaking – and therefore a manner of being – once accepted is already unacceptable.

By Ionesco's argument, even the most contemporary form is 'already tottering and yawning with unsuspected cracks'. That which today appears vital and innovative will tomorrow have already begun to lose its ability to challenge, to penetrate, to effect. The artist requires circumstances in which to create work which is not necessarily popular, and almost certainly not commercially viable.

Performance work must be allowed to create its own terms. Performance, like other forms of art, cannot be tailored to meet demands – whether of the audience or those of the funding bodies. An artist cannot work to the expectations of others *and* also create honest expressions of herself. This means that work cannot be expected to fit into preconceived patterns – even if those patterns do ensure funding, or audiences, or critical success.

What is more, preconceived patterns tend, on the whole, to conform to the 'myth of popularity'. The avant-garde, innovative, or unconventional artist is deemed inaccessible, inappropriate, unpopular – yet as Ionesco, again, put it:

> The so-called popular theatre is actually far more unpopular. It is a theatre which is arrogantly imposed throughout by a ruling aristocracy, a special class of initiates who know or think they know in advance what the public needs. They even say to the public: 'You must only need what we want you to need and you must only think in the way we think.' Paradoxically, the free work of art, by its individualistic character, despite its unusual appearance, alone springs from men's hearts, through a man's heart: it is the only thing which really expresses the people.

In Britain, theatre and performance work is impoverished because it is, by necessity, compromised. The 'free work of art' has little chance of emerging, and less chance of being nurtured and developed. The majority of the population is alienated from performance as from other forms of art. In place of a live culture, we have a commercial system which peddles entertainments designed to attract audiences, funding, and the attention of the press. It is little wonder that most people have no interest in art: art has no genuine interest in them either.

New Journal for Latin American Cultural Studies

A NEW JOURNAL of Latin American cultural studies, *Travesia*, is now being published twice yearly by the Centre for Latin American Cultural Studies, King's College, London. The first issue of Volume I (1992), contains a valuable and highly critical article by Catherine Boyle on the significance of Ariel Dorfman's *Death and the Maiden* in London and Chile, and a translation of Griseldo Gambaro's play *Loose Ends*, from Argentina. Single issues are available at £5 for individuals and £10 for institutions.

Enquiries should be addressed to: Dr. John Kraniauskas, Department of Spanish and Latin American Studies, Birkbeck College, Malet Sreet, London WC1E 7HX.

Shakespeare on the Stage 1900-45

THE University of Leicester will be sponsoring its third theatre conference from 15 to 17 July 1994 on the theme of 'Shakespeare on the Stage 1900-45'. Proposals for papers are invited: their scope might encompass the continuing pictorial tradition of the Victorian actor-managers, William Poel, Granville Barker, the Old Vic, the Shakespeare Memorial Theatre, modern-dress Shakespeare, and the early careers of Gielgud, Olivier, and Guthrie. Papers on Shakespeare on the provincial, North American, and European stage will also be welcomed. The programme will be finalized in the summer of 1993.

Enquiries, or proposals for papers (which should include a synopsis of not more than 500 words) should be addressed to: Richard Foulkes, Conference Director, 'Shakespeare on the Stage 1900-45', Department of Adult Education, University of Leicester, University Road, Leicester LE1 7RH.

NTQ Book Reviews
edited by Viv Gardner

Theatre History to 1900

Marianne McDonald
Ancient Sun, Modern Light:
Greek Drama on the Modern Stage
New York: Columbia University Press, 1992.
239 p.
ISBN 0-231-07654-1.

The title is slightly misleading, in that this book deals with free adaptations of Greek tragedy rather than orthodox productions. McDonald examines work by Suzuki Tadashi, Peter Sellars, Tony Harrison (*Trackers* and *Medea*), Theodoros Terzopoulos (directing Muller), and Thomas Murphy. Interviews with Harrison and Murphy and talks by Sellars and Terzopoulos are incorporated as chapters. McDonald's thesis is that 'Our past has shaped our present, and our present reshapes our past. Modern reworkings of ancient drama help inform the present' (p. 201). After reading this book, I was more informed about the present than about the past refracted through the present. For my taste, the book is too eclectic in its methodology, and focuses too much upon the content of ancient plays at the expense of their dramaturgy, but it does document an important body of modern experimentation.

DAVID WILES

Malveena McKendrick
Theatre in Spain 1490-1700
Cambridge: Cambridge University Press, 1992.
330 p. £14.95.
ISBN 0-521-42901-3.

The publication of the paperback edition of this excellent critical survey of Spanish Golden Age theatre comes at a particularly opportune moment, when the recognition afforded to dramatists like Lope de Vega, Tirso de Molina, and Calderón is no longer merely formal, but is beginning to develop as a meaningful evaluation of the quality of their plays in performance. McKendrick's book does these writers full justice, providing important insights both of a comparative and specific nature. Most importantly, her analysis is grounded in the awareness that here were professional dramatists who worked with a specific audience in mind, and whose creative thinking was predicated on a very real sense of stage dynamics.

Of course, the Spanish Golden Age possessed a richness which goes beyond the vast output of these three major players, and McKendrick displays great critical skill in her tracing of the rise and subsequent flowering of the Spanish drama in all its range and complexity. This is a book which Hispanists and professional theatre practitioners alike will find of great interest, and which will accordingly make its own contribution to the ever growing repertoire of Spanish classical plays in performance.

DAVID JOHNSTON

Gotz Pochat
Theater und Bildende Kunst im Mittelalter
und in der Renaissance in Italien
Graz: Akademische Druck u. Verlagsanstalt,
1990. x, 434 p.

This concise and authoritative overview by the Professor of Art History at Graz University of the interconnections between theatre and art in Italy during the Middle Ages and the Renaissance will be welcomed by theatre historians, not only for its wealth of illustrations and the impressive standard of their reproduction, but for the highly informative manner in which it traces the various and not always immediately evident links between painting, sculpture, architecture, and performance events.

It avoids sacrificing the high medieval for the more richly documented later centuries, providing from its particular perspective a useful examination of the still rather under-explored Italian medieval theatre. Short chapter sections address the rich variety of medieval dramatic and theatrical kinds, through the mimes, *ioculatores*, and *contrasti*, to the religious drama: and although illustration here of the more 'popular' forms is rather thin, the text compensates by examining the complexities of the relationship of these to the religious stages.

Although Pochat appropriately includes some of the more familiar northern visual evidence, like that from Hildesheim and Valenciennes, he focuses more particularly on Italian illustrative materials, notably those bearing on the *laude drammatiche* and the *sacre rappresentazioni*. There are good discussions of these, in relation both to painting and the literary texts, and very good documentation of the later Brunelleschi stagings in the SS. Annuziata and S. Felice in Piazza.

Indeed, throughout the book there is much suggestive juxtaposition of text, drawing, painting, and fresco evidence to illuminate many areas and kinds of stage appearance and practice: thus although acting styles and on-stage action are not Pochat's specific concerns, the illustrative material he has assembled is often suggestive – as, for example, are the strikingly familiar scenes in the work of Bartolomeo della Gatta.

Pochat's terminal date for the Renaissance is *c.* 1530-40: he closes his discussion of the connections between art and stage decoration with the early sixteenth century materials illustrative of the new perspective staging, and his account of theatre architecture runs through to the work of Palladio and Scamozzi at the end of the century. One advantage of this restraint is that the seminal developments of the fifteenth century – the flowering of the *sacre rappresentazioni*, the humanist academy and court recuperations and innovations of the second half of the century, and the development of festival paratheatricals – get detailed coverage. The visual documentation here includes virtually all the important evidence, there is a very balanced account of the transmission of classical materials to the Italian humanists, and allied celebratory activities are well explored – fifteenth century *trionfi* in particular getting extensive treatment.

In his commentary Pochat cites all the Italian texts in the original, with German translations, and there are several useful appendices, including inventories of artefacts from the early fifteenth century confraternities of Assisi and Perugia, and a chronology of performances and *feste* between 1200 and 1598. There is an excellently detailed bibliography, and the whole is thoroughly indexed. This will be a standard work of reference and a useful research tool.

KEN RICHARDS

Ralph Berry
The Methuen Book of Shakespeare Anecdotes
London: Methuen, 1992. £15.99.
ISBN 0-413-66500-3.

Unlike Diana Rigg's *No Turn Unstoned* and Ned Sherrin's *Theatrical Anecdotes*, Berry's book is not one in which to dip for gossip or a giggle. It is concerned solely with Shakespeare on stage and casts its net widely from the sixteenth to the twentieth century. Trawling through five centuries renders the catch (in only 205 pages) a very selective one. Many of the anecdotes are quite serious comments on actors and productions: few of them are calculated to raise a guffaw.

Does this make the book too serious or, dare one say it, too dull? Hardly. The Bard on stage can certainly provide material for amusement, though his usual tone is one of wry humour in comedy and on more serious matters sad reflection. For the academic working in Theatre Studies, few of the anecdotes chronicled here are unknown.

In a way this is a curious book. For whom is it intended? It is not exactly a source-book to which one would turn for, say, an anecdote about a particular Shakespeare play (the entries are limited) nor will it provide comment on a large number of modern Shakespeare actors or directors. But then it is not meant to be an encyclopedia. I rather suspect the book is a result of this distinguished writer's years of research on Shakespeare in the theatre – items he is loath to leave in his card index cabinet unused.

For the general reader the book will be a delight; for the cognoscenti it will remind them of half-forgotten stories; for most readers it will provide something of interest. Ralph Berry is an academic who writes eminently readable books on Shakespeare and other Elizabethan dramatists: read his *Changing Styles in Shakespeare* before expending your hard earned money on this one.

PHILIP S. COOK

Twentieth-Century Theatre

Anna Micinska
Witkacy: Life and Work
Warsaw: Interpress; London: Orbis Books, 1990.
368 p. £25.00.
ISBN 83-223-2359-X.

It was not until the late 1960s and the 1970s that Witkiewicz's plays and writings became known in the West, largely through the translations of his work by Daniel Gerould. In Britain productions of the plays are still few and far between, in spite of the growing availability of texts and critical material. In an age of political disillusionment, a writer who in his life deplored the destructive effects on the human spirit of all forms of socialization might yet experience a revival. Certainly the plays are funny, and are full of formal innovations and devices – and much poorer playwrights achieved eminence when the Theatre of the Absurd was in vogue. Witkiewicz, who predated the Absurd by some twenty or thirty years, might yet be recognized as the most talented and serious writer to be included in that movement, and is certainly its greatest theorist.

This book is a lavish compilation covering all aspects of his remarkable career, and is replete with illustrations, including a mass of Witkiewicz's own photographs and colour reproductions of his paintings and drawings. In covering all aspects of Witkacy's work, life, and the society of his times, the book manages to combine an indispensable work of scholarship with a coffee-table standard of presentation, which will impress all who call on you, for only £25.

CLIVE BARKER

Drewey Wayne Gunn
Tennessee Williams: a Bibliography
Metuchen, N.J.: Scarecrow Press, 1991. 434 p.
£37.15.
ISBN 0-8108-2495-7.

The decade which has elapsed since the appearance of Professor Gunn's first edition has, sadly, seen the demise of his bibliography's prolific and celebrated subject. Tennessee Williams's death in 1983 prompted an enormous amount of retrospective analysis, critical commentary, new productions, and a general revival of interest in the canon, all of which activity is comprehensively documented in this second edition, along with pre-1980 material.

Every effort has been made in the new edition not only to create an exhaustive listing of plays, screenplays, short stories, novels, poems, lyrics, autobiography, letters, recordings, and biographical sources and interviews, but also to provide the user with a cross-referencing system which allows threads to be followed between discrete sections. In addition, an excellent index of human subjects (actors, directors, musicians, critics) provides hundreds of points of entry into the listings.

Of particular interest to the theatre scholar will be Gunn's compilation of translations and foreign-language productions. Until such time as on-line search facilities and CD-Rom supported databases create keyboard and monitor retrieval systems for this kind of extensive bibliographical material, and probably for long after, Professor Gunn's volume will be an indispensable asset to anyone with more than a passing interest in the life and work of Tennessee Williams.

CHRIS BANFIELD

Brenda Murphy
Tennessee Williams and Elia Kazan
Cambridge University Press, 1992. 201 p. £25.95.
ISBN 0-521-40095-3.

Eric Bentley's testing critique of *Camino Real* following its Broadway opening in 1953 raised an ironic question mark not only over the extent of Tennessee Williams's contribution to Kazan's production of the play but, in identifying Kazan's creative hand in an earlier landmark of modern American drama, *A Streetcar Named Desire* (1947), also posited the notion that hitherto accepted conventions of the integrity of the playwright's artistic vision might have to include an acceptance of directorial influence in collaborative processes which created the theatrical event. Such criticism was fiercely contested by Williams, who, in spite of resentments throughout their volatile relationship, had still sought Kazan's authority over most of his plays since *Streetcar*.

An inconclusive fracture occurred following Williams's allegation that Kazan's interference with *Cat on a Hot Tin Roof* was for 'commercial' motives.

Professor Murphy selects four collaborations between Williams and the Actors' Studio guru (*Sweet Bird of Youth* making up the quartet), meticulously exploring aspects of their involvement in pre-production, design, casting, rehearsals, performance and critical response. What is most evident is the staggering industry with which Williams continually redrafted to meet his director's demands, together with Kazan's methodically ruthless approach to eliciting a kinesic language of performance from Brando *et al.*

CHRIS BANFIELD

Sean O'Casey
Niall: a Lament
London: Calder; New York: Riverrun, 1991. 96 p.
£14.99.
ISBN 0-7145-4196-6.

This private diary from the pen of Sean O'Casey was clearly never intended for publication, and will never sit comfortably in the public arena of drama studies. In 1956 Niall O'Casey, the son of the playwright, died from leukaemia at the age of only 21. The diary covers the period from 1956 to 1960, and records the painful, reluctant, and ultimately uncompleted process of the father letting go of the son. There are glimpses into the author's agnosticism, pacifistic inclination, and sincere humanity: but all these qualities are well documented elsewhere, and resonate throughout the plays. The diary was only discovered in 1964 following Sean O'Casey's death, and Eileen O'Casey withheld authorization for publication at the time. It is difficult to understand why, if this document was 'far too poignant' then, it is any the less so now. It records an intensely private grief and clearly should have remained private.

PADRAIG TOLAN

John Osborne
Almost a Gentleman: an Autobiography
Vol. II, 1955-1966
London: Faber, 1991. 283 p. £14.99.
ISBN 0-571-16261-4.

John Osborne's second volume of autobiography has achieved some notoriety through the excerpts published in the Sunday papers. These were almost entirely taken up with his various marriages and extra-marital relationships, and, through an unfortunate coincidence, his critical assessment of a former colleague, Tony Richardson, appeared almost simultaneously with the latter's obituary notices. It would be a great pity, however, if this book were ignored through false impressions aroused by pre-publicity, for there is much generosity here towards his contemporaries and fellow writers: indeed, having lived through the period, I find Osborne's valuation of many of our contemporaries much more generous and restrained than mine would be.

The book is full of insights into the theatre of the ten year period after the 'breakthrough'. It is Osborne's own story, but that is an important part of the overall history. If he cuts through the legends and the hype to show the hypocrisy, small-mindedness, and destructive egoism of those times, then that, too, is an important part of the history. Ignore the marital detail if you like: but read the theatre history, it's well worth it.

CLIVE BARKER

D. *Keith Peacock*
Radical Stages:
Alternative History in Modern British Drama
Connecticut: Greenwood Press, 1991. 202 p.
£34.40.
ISBN 0-313-27888-1.

Keith Peacock's work focuses on the way in which history has been used and abused by British playwrights from (in Part I) 1956 to 1968 and (in the longer Part II) 1968 to 1984, in an attempt to demonstrate that for writers of British historical drama 'all history was to become *contemporary* history'. It is a subject fraught with difficulties – most notably of the ideological variety – as the author continually acknowledges; and the tension between the urge to discuss the issues involved in any 'construction' of history and the attempt to present notes towards a mapping of the changes and developments in the dramatic presentation and use of such constructions results in a frequently tentative approach. Theatrical movements, texts, and authors come and go in a series of too brief skirmishes with political movements, events, and actors, the whole thing overshadowed by the never properly discussed problematics of historiography.

The book's concern with both history and drama makes its omissions doubly problematic. It is an area of debate as fascinating and important as it is contentious, and, considering the existence of a major contemporary debate in the (in this instance at least) related disciplines of history, literature, and drama about the construction and deconstruction of historical/fictional 'realities', it is disturbing to note that the only modernish theorist to receive even a mention comes with the briefest of glancing references to Georg Lukacs.

The book is ultimately more concerned with the plays than with the intellectual framework that gives the book its supposed *raison d'être*, but

the lack of any consistently developed methodology gives the cataloguing of texts a rather arbitrary feeling. A concentration in Part II on writers in whose work can be found a construction of history on the 'radical' or 'alternative' terms that are incorporated into the book's title sits very uneasily, for instance, with the more general scope of a Part I that is able to take time out to perform the arduous task of demonstrating that Robert Bolt's *A Man For All Seasons* and John Osborne's *Luther* are not, properly speaking, Brechtian plays. The result is a confusion that seems to arise from an uncertainty about the nature of the task rather than from the inevitable complexities of the subject considered in real depth. Ultimately the book is neither a general overview of the problems raised by the use of history by dramatists across the entire political spectrum, nor a particular view from the left, although it seems at times to offer both.

JOHN BULL

Simon *Reade*
Cheek by Jowl: Ten Years of Celebration
Bath: Absolute Classics, 1991. 135 p. £9.95.
ISBN 0-948230-49-5.

In Brazil they are called *Rosto a Rosto* (Face to Face), in Argentina *Codo con Codo* (Elbow to Elbow), in Spain *Carne y Uña* (Flesh and Nail): in the UK we recognize them as Cheek by Jowl, one of the more adventurous of theatre companies. It is apparent they tour a lot, especially abroad, but they like to take theatre to places not overserved with resident drama groups. They have now been in existence for a decade – hence this celebratory paperback detailing their beginnings and recording their achievements. It is no mean feat in today's theatre climate for a new theatre company dedicated to small-scale touring not only to have lasted ten years, but also to have carved out a name for consistent high standards, while upgrading themselves to a middle-scale touring company. Cause for celebration indeed.

Cheek by Jowl opened in 1981 with *The Country Wife*, and they have since gone on to produce classics from the Greek, English, Spanish, and French Golden Ages of theatre. Theirs is not the modern theatre of journalism: they tangle only with the best. Led by Declan Donnellan and Nick Omerod, Cambridge graduates who read law and almost immediately eschewed the bar for the stage, this director-designer duo, together with the administrative expertise of Barbara Matthews, has lasted the course, and is still set fair for the future. It says much for the group's status that they have been chosen to represent Great Britain in Spain this year at Expo '92, and that Donnellan and Omerod have now presented two shows in London at the Royal National Theatre.

The secret of their success lies in an astute choice of repertoire and a belief in ensemble theatre. Theatre to them is first and foremost a place of emotional truth and vivid storytelling. As Simon Reade observes, 'To use theatre as a provocative, political medium, you first have to reclaim theatre.' Over the years, the same team of director, designer, administrator, advisers on movement and music, and in several cases the same actors, have rethought theatre and reforged the classics, weaving their theatrical spells from Aberdeen to Wallingford and from Adelaide to Zutphen.

Naturally not everyone has been spellbound all the time. Their *Hamlet* was mauled as 'something . . . rockin'' in the state of Denmark', while their version of *El Cid* was described by one critic as *Cid Vicious*. But such comments are far outweighed by the obvious delight with which most of their work has been received. If you saw *Fuente Ovejuna* at the National you will appreciate their impact. This book is a fair and data-filled factual record of their progress to date.

PHILIP S. COOK

Penina Muhando Mlama
Culture and Development:
the Popular Theatre Approach in Africa.
Uppsala: Scandinavian Institute of African Studies, 1991. 219 p.
ISBN 91-7106-317-X.

This book is an important contribution to the still slim body of published work on developments in African theatre. *Culture and Development* starts with macro-considerations of the role of culture, and specifically theatre, in the development process, and gradually focuses on specific projects in various African nations before examining in depth three initiatives in Tanzania.

Much of what Penina Muhando Mlama says about the perils of neglecting the cultural factor in development debates is hardly new, even though the message has been slow in reaching government and aid agencies. However, the author raises interesting points concerning important questions, such as the kinds of cultural production which can be included in popular theatre; who should play the role of animateur; and how to give a voice to the weaker sections of any given community.

This study is greatly enriched by the fact that nearly all Muhando Mlama's material draws on first-hand experience of the workshops she describes. I did feel that particularly in the Tanzanian case studies the author failed to give sufficient weight to the impact several high-powered academics might have had in persuading government officials to act on local problems, as opposed to village-power mobilized through theatre.

Also one would have liked to know what happened to the theatre groups after the animateurs went away. In spite of these reservations, *Culture and Development* must be essential reading for all those concerned with popular theatre in the Third World.

JANE PLASTOW

Performance, Theory, General Studies

Michael J. Sidnell, ed.
Sources of Dramatic Theory:
1, Plato to Congreve
Cambridge: Cambridge University Press, 1991. 317 p.
ISBN 0-521-3269-4.

Filling in many gaps in theatrical theory from the Greeks to the Renaissance, this collection of writings – the first in a four-volume series – encompasses the work of a wide variety of theatrical practitioners and essayists. As well as segments from the better-known theatrical writings of Plato, Aristotle, Jonson, Corneille, Racine, Dryden, and Congreve, Michael J. Sidnell has included Lope de Vega's 'New Art of Making Comedias' and an extract from Tirso de Molina's 'The Country Houses of Toledo' – both crucial texts for any understanding of the Spanish Golden Age theatre – as well as material by Lorenzo Giacomini and Sforza Oddi. Each of the thirty extracts is contextualized and accompanied by detailed notes, there is a comprehensive bibliography, and an overview of the period is provided by Sidnell's concise but informative introduction. A number of the extracts appear in English for the first time, and Sidnell is to be commended for the range of European texts provided. An invaluable sourcebook to complement any study of the plays of the period and the conditions in which they were performed.

MARIA M. DELGADO

Murray Cox, ed.
Shakespeare Comes to Broadmoor: the Performance of Tragedy in a Secure Psychiatric Hospital
London: Jessica Kingsley, 1992. 282 p.
ISBN 0-85302-135-0.

There is, as Ian McKellen says in his introduction, no need to apologize for this further addition to the Shakespeare criticism industry. Although full of critical insights into Shakespearean tragedy, this book is actually about the Broadmoor audience who are placed quite firmly at centre stage – not only to be written about at length by the many contributors, but also providing the most interesting chapter as the patients comment in their own words about the performances of *Hamlet*, *King Lear*, and *Romeo and Juliet* that were performed by the RSC at Broadmoor Hospital over the last three years.

The book is important not only because it chronicles work that needs to be discussed so that it can be developed further, but because it is vital to our understanding of what theatre does and how it operates in the world outside. Gloriously incomplete and rough-hewn, the book leaves the reader to do much of the work, matching one essay against another and trying to find difficult answers to questions that are still being formulated.

As Murray Cox states, there is little literature or research to support and sustain those engaged in drama in a custodial setting, and it is to be hoped that this book is just a beginning. Reports and thoughts from forensic psychiatrists, dramatherapists, psychodramatists, and psychiatric nurses are complemented from the theatrical side by, amongst others, Brian Cox, Clare Higgins, Mark Rylance, Deborah Warner, Saul Hewish (Artistic Director of Geese Theatre), and the robust Cicely Berry, whose chapter combines the detail of practice with a vital sense of vision and purpose.

PAUL HERITAGE

Frederick Burwick
Illusion and the Drama: Critical
Theory of the Enlightenment and Romantic Era
Pennsylvania: Pennsylvania State University Press, 1991. 326 p. £28.00.
ISBN 0-271-00732-X.

This volume analyzes attitudes towards illusionism in French, German, and English dramatic criticism of the eighteenth and early nineteenth century. The author has selected a representative range of critics and subdivided their views conveniently with regard to acting (Diderot and Tieck), audience response (Mendelssohn and Lessing), playwriting (Schlegel and Coleridge), stage design (Goethe and Hugo), and metadrama (Coleridge and Tieck).

The book, written from the perspective of a literary historian, makes very few references to theatre practice or, in fact, to the wider framework of the other arts and the philosophy of the period. Although, in his introductory chapter, the author attempts to outline the significance of illusionism in twentieth-century aesthetic debates, his short summaries of the theories of Adorno, Husserl, Gadamer, *et al.* are not complemented by any discussion of the role of illusionism in the theatre of our time, especially in the naturalist tradition from Stanislavsky to Strasberg. Given the time limits the author has imposed on himself

such omissions may be justified: however, our understanding of the eighteenth- and nineteenth-century critics to whom the study is dedicated would also have benefited from a placing of their theories in the context of the staging conventions of the time.

The same applies to the philosophical discourses in the fields of aesthetics and epistemology which formed the basis of any inquiry into the nature of illusion and its role in the cognitive and creative process. Two and a half pages on Kant and Hegel do not suffice for this purpose. And what about Locke and Hume, or Fichte and Schelling, whose theories were of paramount importance to the concept of illusionism in the Enlightenment and Romantic era respectively?

Equally, the reader would have benefited from an analysis of how the theories dealt with in the main chapters grew out of and reacted against the tradition of theatrical artifice on the Baroque stage. After all, an Italianate 'theatre of illusion' had been in existence for a good 150 years, and continued to be practised not only in small and insignificant residential theatres, but also at the Burgtheater in Vienna, the Hof- und Staatstheater in Berlin and Dresden, and the Académie de Musique in Paris. An important task in this enquiry would have been to analyze how the new theories of illusionism related to the older traditions, and how the great theatrical innovations of the Romantics (Tieck in Berlin, Hoffmann in Bamberg, Immermann in Dusseldorf) were reflected in the drama criticism of the period.

None of this, unfortunately, may be found in this rather self-enclosed and selective study. As a result, the book may satisfy a reader who wishes to consult a compartmentalized, heuristic exposition of some key theories of the period, but a comparative approach would have led to more fruitful results and more productive insights.

GÜNTER BERGHAUS

David Hornbrook
Education in Drama:
Casting the Dramatic Curriculum
London: Falmer Press, 1991. 181 p. £10.95.
ISBN 1-85000-721-7.

This is a book that will annoy immensely those who are hostile to the National Curriculum and any attempt to fit drama into its rigid schema, and please others for its hard-headed determination to put the case, practically and theoretically, for the subject as a viable and necessary part of any balanced curriculum provision within our schools.

Following hard upon the heels of Hornbrook's previous book, *Education and Dramatic Art*, this offers what many complained was lacking in the first – a practical set of guidelines for how a dramatic curriculum might be introduced, structured, and assessed both in primary and secondary schools. It acknowledges that the National Curriculum is here for the foreseeable future, and that drama's exclusion from it is an unacceptable state of affairs. To justify the subject in its own right (rather than, as now, an adjunct to English), Hornbrook argues that we must pull back from therapeutic and pedagogical models of drama teaching and reassert the subject's *theatrical* roots. We have to evolve a model and language for educational drama that derives from theatrical practice in the broadest sense, and focus upon what he (persuasively) argues should be three main 'attainment targets' – those of 'Making', 'Performing', and 'Responding'.

The case Hornbrook makes for drama as a viable and discrete subject in schools is coherent, cogent, and comprehensible. The main drawback (and it is a fundamental one) is that, when he moves on to articulate what this means in terms of objectives, skills, tasks, and levels of work as required by the National Curriculum's current framework, he ends up by accentuating skills and product throughout at the expense of the creative learning *process*. Gone (it seems) is the use of drama to examine the world of things, relationships, and feelings: technique has become all.

ANTHONY JACKSON

Peter Barkworth
The Complete About Acting
London: Methuen Drama, 1991. 274 p. £8.99.
ISBN 0-413-66110-5.

This new edition combines *About Acting* (1980) and *More About Acting* (1984) with a little updating in the form of 1991 postscripts and one additional interview. Aimed at the budding or jobbing mainstream actor or actress, it is more, in the author's own words, a series of 'helpful hints and golden rules' for stage, TV, and film acting than a probe into the depth of the creative processes of performance or discovery of forms of expression.

The tips are most useful when most concrete – 'if you breathe in before you drink you cannot choke' – although they engage some larger issues productively as well, such as the way to keep a performance fresh by varying the circumstances or changing the point of concentration. The reconciliation of repetition and spontaneity is always at the core of the acting process, and there are some effective pointers here. Other recommendations, however, like learning lines before rehearsals (!) and taking predetermined moves from directors (recanted in a 1991 postscript) are old-fashioned and counterproductive.

What the book does best, through lively anecdotes and quotes from acting colleagues, is

to convey a full feeling of the jobbing actor's life and working solutions. The interviews (with Dench, McCowan, Massey, Rees, and Scales, among others), triggered well by Barkworth's engaging style, are the high points, with Alison Steadman's account of building her role in *Abigal's Party* a complete revelation about acting.

ALAN PEARLMAN

Books Received

Notice in this column does not preclude the possibility of review in a later issue.

History, Criticism, Theory

Peter Branscombe, *W. A. Mozart: Die Zauberflöte*. Cambridge: Cambridge University Press, 1991. £30.00 (hbk), £9.95 (pbk). (Cambridge Opera Handbooks.)

Douglas Jarman, *Alban Berg: Lulu*. Cambridge: Cambridge University Press, 1991. £27.50 (hbk), £9.95 (pbk). (Cambridge Opera Handbooks.)

John MacKenzie, *Popular Imperialism and the Military*. Manchester: Manchester University Press, 1992. £35.00.

Wendy Trewin, *The Royal General Theatrical Fund*. London: Society for Theatre Research, 1989.

Raymond Williams, *Drama in Performance*. Reprinted from the 1968 edition, with new introduction and bibliography by Graham Holderness. Milton Keynes: Open University Press, 1991. £9.99.

'Writer-Files' Series, gen. ed. Simon Trussler: *File on Edgar*, ed. Malcolm Page and Simon Trussler (London: Methuen, 1991. £5.99); *File on Mamet*, ed. Nesta Jones and Steven Dykes (London: Methuen, 1991. £5.99).

Plays

Jean Anouilh, *The Rehearsal*, trans. Jeremy Sams. London: Methuen, 1991. £4.99.

Edward Bond, *The War Plays*. London: Methuen, 1991. £9.99. [Includes *Red, Black, and Ignorant, Great Peace*.]

Calderón, *Plays: One*, trans. Gwynne Edwards. London: Methuen, 1991. £6.99. [Includes *The Surgeon of Honour, Life is a Dream, Three Judgements in One*.]

Jim Cartwright, *To*. London: Methuen, 1991. £4.99.

Jim Cartwright, *Bed*. London: Methuen, 1991. £4.99.

Caryl Churchill, *Top Girls*. London: Methuen 1991. £4.99. (Methuen Student Editions.)

Euripides, *Hecuba*, trans.Jeanet Rembke and Kenneth J. Reckford. Oxford University Press, 1991. £25.00 (hbk), £4.99 (pbk).